D0227018

 libraries

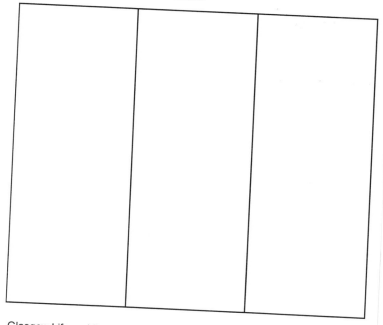

Visit our How To website at **www.howto.co.uk**

At **www.howto.co.uk** you can engage in conversation with our authors - all of whom have 'been there and done that' in their specialist fields. You can get access to special offers and additional content but most importantly you will be able to engage with, and become a part of, a wide and growing community of people just like yourself.

At **www.howto.co.uk** you'll be able to talk and share tips with people who have similar interests and are facing similar challenges in their lives. People who, just like you, have the desire to change their lives for the better - be it through moving to a new country, starting a new business, growing their own vegetables, or writing a novel.

At **www.howto.co.uk** you'll find the support and encouragement you need to help make your aspirations a reality.

You can go direct to **www.challenging-depression-and-despair.co.uk** which is part of the main How To site.

How To Books strives to present authentic, inspiring, practical information in their books. Now, when you buy a title from How To Books, you get even more than just words on a page.

Challenging Depression and Despair

A medication-free self-help programme that will change your life

Angela Patmore

howto**books**

To my parents

Published by How To Books Ltd,
Spring Hill House, Spring Hill Road,
Begbroke, Oxford OX5 1RX
Tel: (01865) 375794
Fax: (01865) 379162
info@howtobooks.co.uk
www.howtobooks.co.uk

How To Books greatly reduse the carbon footprint of their books by sourcing their
typesetting and printing in the UK.

British Library Cataloguing in Publication Data
A catalogue record for this book is available from the British Library

ISBN 978-1-84528-439-8

Cover design by Baseline Arts Ltd, Oxford
Produced for How To Books by Deer Park Productions, Tavistock, Devon
Typeset by Baseline Arts Ltd, Oxford
Printed and bound in Great Britain by Bell and Bain Ltd, Glasgow

NOTE: The material contained in this book is set out in good faith for general guidance
and no liability can be accepted for loss or expense incurred as a result of relying in
particular circumstances on statements made in the book. The laws and regulations
are complex and liable to change, and readers should check the current position with
the relevant authorities before making personal arrangements.

Contents

Part 2 BEATING DESPAIR: THE CHALLENGES

Introduction

Congratulations on having the courage to choose this book. Even if you were simply attracted by the title, this tells me that there is hope for you. You have the potential to benefit from the contents, because you haven't yet gone belly-up on your condition, as so many in this nannying age have been lulled into doing. It also tells me that the 'softly softly' approach to depression, kind and sympathetic though it may appear, hasn't cured you, and that you are looking for something different.

Well, you've come to the right place. This book is offered as a lifeline to people at the bottom of the bottomless pit of despair. It will explain the research and the thinking behind the 'tough love' approach, much of which may be new to you because it flies in the face of current trends, and it will culminate in a programme of ten challenges that will enable you to change your entire attitude to emotional health. Your self-empowerment will come from the knowledge of the first and the experience of the second.

When I was young, I suffered from suicidal despair, cried for days, sobbed in the street, lost all my self-respect, took an overdose, was dragged back to life and then floundered about for ages through research, training and academic degrees looking for a magic mindset that would make me happy and self-reliant.

I can tell you now that softly-softly therapies, however well intentioned, made me worse. 'Stress management' and avoidant strategies promising protection from serious problems made me helpless. Yet if someone had handed me this book when I was down, I could have been spared years of anguish. Let me save you the trouble I went through. If all else has failed, it's worth a try.

DECLARATION OF EMOTIONAL INDEPENDENCE

There are many books that medicalise your mind. This will not be one of them. Human emotions are what make us tick. The negative ones may be unpleasant, but even these are not without purpose and they are part of our normal development. Cutting-edge science on the brain suggests they are also important to our creative life. Feelings should not be 'pathologised' – turned into a disease. You can learn to *master* your negative emotions by understanding and channelling them. But you do not need a lobotomy.

Books on mental health issues tend to mollycoddle the reader. Well, you won't get any 'tea and sympathy' out of me. I am, to quote the *New Statesman*, 'widely regarded as a heartless bitch'.[1]

THE 'STRESS' OGRESS

My book on 'stress' caused a storm of controversy because it questioned the whole basis of current diagnosis and soothing treatment. Though it was shortlisted for the MIND Book of the Year Award, it did not offer to help manage anybody's 'stress'. What it recommended was removing the whole stress ideology from people's heads like a rotting tooth, so that they could feel normal again, talk about their various feelings and experiences without recourse to a medical dictionary, and find new confidence and courage to face their problems head on.

The Truth About Stress[2] said that spreading 'stress awareness' made people believe they were mentally ill when they were not, and that selling calm-down products and 'expertise' on the basis of this deception was profoundly immoral. It set out to dispel fears about negative emotions and their impact on health, offering empowerment and hope to millions of 'stress' sufferers.

DROWSY NUMBNESS

Unlike 'stress', which covers literally hundreds of different feelings and physiological states, 'depression' generally means just one thing:

A powerful, mind-destroying emptiness
that saps the strength and the will.

If you are depressed you feel as though a light has gone out in your soul. This is what the poet Keats called the 'drowsy numbness that pains the sense'[3] and it is not only disastrous to life but dangerous to health. It should not be mollified with tea and sympathy, but faced down and defeated.

Unfortunately this will not be achieved by my sitting in a pool of tears with you and saying, 'there there, poor soul, you are too delicate for this world – have another pill'. Routing your inner deadness will require courage and intelligence from you, and clear, practical, common sense, evidence-based strategies from me. Although you are unlikely to believe it until you are shown the evidence later on, 'tea and sympathy' and soothing 'stress management' may have helped to get you precisely where you are today.

Theories about abnormal psychology and psychiatry can lead to morbid introspection and self-diagnosis on the part of the patient victim, or the victimised patient. The sufferer may then be trapped in a cycle that confirms his or her status as a 'mental patient' and produces more negative thoughts, more anxiety, more symptoms and more treatment.

For anyone caught in this cycle, a new door is needed at the clinic that says:

WAY OUT AND STAY OUT!

This book will examine 'depression' in a new way. It will not make a syndrome out of your condition. My background is academic research and life skills training. I am not your therapist. You are certainly not my patient. You are therefore not going to be labelled with a medical-sounding name like 'depressive' or 'manic-depressive' or 'bi-polar' or 'cyclothymic'. Your feelings will not be referred to as 'flat affect' or 'clinical depression' or 'SAD (Seasonal Affective Disorder)' or any other term beloved of all those Head Help Honchos out there with authority over your psyche. The simple expression that past generations would have used is to say that you are dejected or 'in despair'. And if you are in despair, you should not be seen as

- a research project

- a guinea pig for psychological theories and treatments

- a market opportunity for 'stress management' firms

- a target for giant pharmaceutical companies

- a 'hopeless case'

- mad.

Interestingly, the UK government recently announced a policy shift over the next ten years that will take a more proactive approach to mental health issues, looking at ways of promoting emotional well-being and personal growth instead of trying to treat millions of syndromes. This book will have the same sunny priorities.

It will aim not merely to sympathise or tranquillise, but to exhilarate. I will offer alternatives to the fashionable calm-down culture that has seen 'stress' and 'depression' statistics skyrocket – creativity, courage, common sense and the sort of life skills with which, as a Department of Employment Restart trainer, I was able to help the long-term unemployed get their lives back together again. These will include techniques and strategies for

- self-empowerment

- problem-solving

- morale-boosting

- improvisation

- facing and conquering fears

- exploiting nervousness

- accepting challenges.

The graduated exercises will be based on research evidence linking mental and physical challenges with emotional health and resilience.

A number of the exercises will involve spontaneity and improvisation. Depressed people find it very hard to act at all, let alone naturally. Yet learning how to be spontaneous can revitalise one's sense of wonder, hope and self-worth. The learning curve will reveal that nervousness is perfectly normal and natural, and that fear and desire are often intimately connected. We may dread situations that are nevertheless important to our goals. This being the case, the only real failure is not to try.

EMBRACING THE REST OF YOUR LIFE
By learning to conquer fear and anxiety rather than seeking to avoid or tranquillise them, you will gradually learn a higher level of emotional strength and self-determination, and you will be able to take a more gung-ho approach to life and life's problems, reducing the need for either chemicals or therapies.

I shall go on to explain the science behind 'toughening up' or inurement, and encourage you to jump out of your present psychological box and accept challenges. Avoidance of fear, tension and pressure, although they may have become a way of life in our 'stress managed' age, are not a way *to* life. In fact everyone actually needs pressure in order to achieve emotional health and operate on all cylinders, and there is sound science to suggest that we live longer if we rush about. It maintains what are known as our heatshock proteins, responsible for keeping cells in good repair and prolonging our lives.

As we shall see, for some people accustomed to avoidance and helplessness, 'depressed' may literally mean '*de*pressed' – having insufficient pressure.

LOOK OUT: DEPRESSED PERSON BEHAVING BADLY!

How do you tell the difference between a person in despair and someone who is not, even before they open their mouths? The despairing person *behaves* differently. Do any of the following seem at all familiar to you?

- **Sleep indiscipline** – sleep a lot, or in the daytime to 'catch up' on lost night-sleep.

- **Avoiding fitness** – not exercising, apart from walking from the car to the shops, school gate, etc. Eating lots of comfort foods containing fat and sugar. Deliberately ruining one's body to show how bad one feels inside.

- **Avoiding work** – can't work, dread work, taking 'sickies' or duvet days.

- **Escaping tasks** – putting off tasks that are difficult, annoying, scary or challenging. Using displacement activities – doing *other* things to avoid the tasks you can't face.

- **Helplessness** – waiting until help arrives, waiting for rescue. *Not* taking the initiative.

- **Self-protection** – avoiding situations that make you feel worried, nervous or 'emotional'.

- **Submissiveness** – allowing yourself to be treated as a doormat.

- **'Eyes down'** – looking at the floor when talking, or the footpath as you walk outside, staring into the little pool of sorrow at your feet.

CHICKEN AND EGG, OR JUST CHICKEN?

Which came first, the strange behaviour or the despair? Depressed people say they behave this way because they are desolate. But habits like these increase feelings of desolation. They may even *cause* them. If normal people adopted these habits, many would almost certainly become depressed.

Now let's look at the comparative *non*-despairing behaviour:

- **Regular sleep** – getting up at a set time each day (with an alarm clock if necessary) and going to bed at more or less the same time each night. *Avoiding* daylight snoozing (known as 'practising sleep hygiene'), even when tired. Most people experience sleepless nights occasionally while the brain works on a particular problem. The more regular sleep rhythm returns in due course.

- **Embracing fitness** –– not to sculpture the body to some ideal shape but simply to *feel* healthy. Exercising at home, taking regular walks or going to a gym, 'park and walk'. Eating lots of fruit and vegetables, cutting out fatty and sugary foods.

- **Embracing work** – taking a pride in one's work, doing the best job possible, thinking of new and better ways of doing one's job, enjoying being useful, finishing what one has started.

- **Tackling rotten tasks** – 'getting on with it', getting things done and dusted, getting them over with.

- **Self-reliance and self-rescue** – Taking the initiative. 'I'll do it myself. If it's something I can't do by myself, I'll ask for assistance. I'm not just sitting here waiting for rescue, as this would annoy me.'

- **Embracing challenges** – doing difficult, scary things that make you excited and exhilarated because they provide a buzz when you've done them.

- **Assertiveness** – saying courteously and considerately what you want and when you want it. Saying 'no' if you don't want it. Courteously repeating yourself if they didn't get you the first time. No need for growing resentment or aggression or 'scenes' if you are assertive in the first place.

- **Eyes on the world** – looking at the person you are speaking to, looking around you when you go out, looking at people's faces, having a curious approach to what's going on out there.

By slowly switching from the first set of habits to the second set, you will notice your mood begin to lift and lighten. You don't have to try them all at once – just one or two that capture your imagination. Human beings were never meant to be negative and avoidant. That's why we were given brains.

Avoidance and indiscipline may be fashionable, and there may be more opportunities for avoidant and sloppy behaviour now than previous generations enjoyed, but escapist and lazy habits don't make people emotionally more robust, or more content, or more cheerful. They make them more scared and cowardly and miserable, because they destroy the brain's interaction with the world.

This is your Heartless Bitch talking. Straighten up and fly right!

NOTES

1. Zoe Williams, 'All too much', *New Statesman*, 13 February 2006.

2. Angela Patmore, *The Truth About Stress*. Grove Atlantic, 2006.

3. 'Ode to a Nightingale', John Keats.

The Author

For nearly four years Angela Patmore was a life skills trainer with the Department of Employment's Restart programme for the long-term unemployed in Colchester. During her tenure the small company for which she worked, Mojo Associates, enjoyed a better outcomes record than all of the region's other training providers combined.

She is the author of books on a variety of subjects but is mainly known as a social issues writer. She produced one of the earliest books on sports psychology in the UK, *Playing on their Nerves*, and was the official biographer of Britain's first and most famous agony aunt, Marje Proops. As part of her research Angela was given access to Marje's two million readers' letters stored in the *Daily Mirror* archives.

Her last book, *The Truth About Stress* (Grove Atlantic, 2006) was shortlisted for the MIND Book of the Year Award.

Angela is a former International Fulbright Scholar with a first-class honours degree in English and a Masters from the College of William and Mary, Virginia. As a University of East Anglia research fellow at the Centre for Environmental Risk (a World Health Organisation collaborating centre) she worked with scientists to produce a meta-analysis of the research literature on 'stress' that gave rise to the 1998 London conference, 'Stress – A Change of Direction'. The conference attracted over sixty national newspaper and television features and brought together critics of 'stress management' from medicine and the sciences, from psychology, the emergency services and the arts.

Under the chairmanship of former Metropolitan Police Commissioner Sir John Stevens, she has also served as a member of the External Experts' Advisory Group on 'stress'.

Part 1

Conquering depression: The knowledge

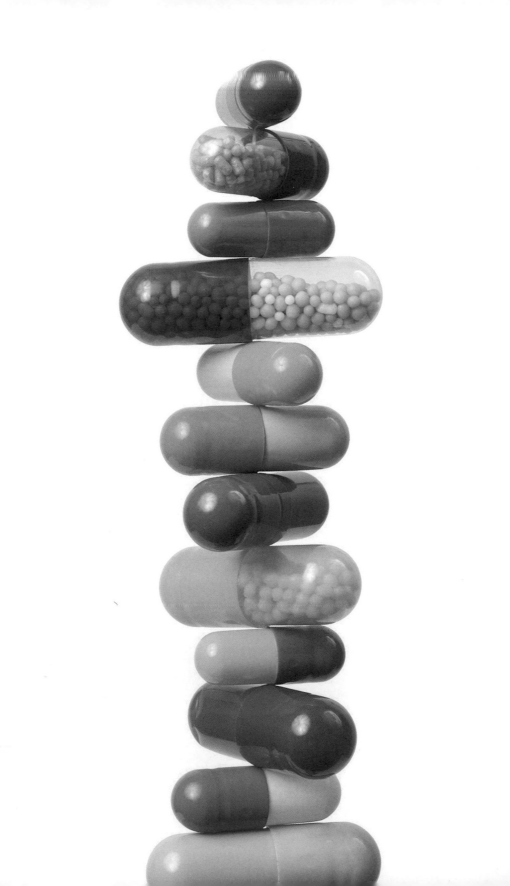

Drugs for despair

So you want help with 'depression,' do you? Maybe you've tried everything else That wouldn't surprise me. For years I've been researching therapies and scientific studies on mental health issues and if I were you, I'd be looking for something different as well. Sigmund Freud once let slip to a friend that his patients were 'only riffraff'.[1] Although some therapists may be a bit more caring and prefer the term 'client' rather than 'patient', at the end of a hard day's therapeutic endeavours the sufferer is still seen as a case (or even nutcase) with a syndrome, symptoms, treatment options, a prognosis. So what else is there?

'PULL YOURSELF TOGETHER'

Pull yourself together. We've all heard it. When you feel down and out, somebody puts the boot in and says this. You may not like it and they may be insensitive, but they are right in one respect. If there is to be any pulling together, *you* have to do the pulling. The cavalry is not coming. Nobody is going to rescue you. Either you're going to help yourself and get better, grow as a person and turn your life around, or you are stuck in a very bad place, annoying more robust people with your dismal attitude. This is the Heartless Bitch talking, but at least I'm giving it to you straight. It's up to you.

In this first part we shall be looking at what has gone wrong with our emotional well-being, why so many people are depressed and despondent, and what we can do about it. We need to get you away from the fashionable 'calm down' culture and pseudo-medical twaddle that goes by the name of 'stress management' because despair may actually result from

- a sedative lifestyle (the constant search for calm)
- false labelling (giving 'syndrome' labels to normal emotions and states)
- medicalising of feelings (like anger, worry, frustration or fear) and
- timid and avoidant attitudes towards negative emotions.

Sure, people in the past suffered from despair, but not in the epidemic numbers that we do nowadays. They had very different ideas on tackling it as well.

Tackling tip: The law of momentum

Here is a useful tip for 'getting going again' if your motivation and adrenalin cease to flow. When children are learning to ride a bike, they quickly discover the law of momentum. If you stop pedalling, the bike keels over and you fall off. You need to keep pedalling, keep moving, even if you're not sure exactly where yet! So it is with mental energy. If you stop taking action, you disengage the brain and it idles. You fall flat. Keep taking action! Even if it is something as simple as 'get out of bed and clean your teeth' or 'clear out that cupboard' or 'make a list of what needs doing', your brain's first gear is engaged, and will gradually move you on from there.

Let's start by looking at the most *common* method of treating despair today.

'OUT OF THE MEDICINE CHEST INTO THE MOUTH'

Medicalising depression is part of the problem that modern sufferers face. Medical diagnosis does two things: first, it implies that you are mentally ill and therefore a patient, psychologically abnormal and possibly mad – compounding your misery and low self-esteem and increasing the likelihood that you will rely on others for help and rescue. And second, diagnosis holds out the hope of a medical solution. That may not be forthcoming.

Doctors are very busy. They haven't got time to talk to you at length about your feelings. What would you do if one in three of your patients came in with this same 'complaint'? The giant chemical companies command trends in research, publication and treatment.

They therefore influence your doctor's methods of dealing with 'patients' like you who 'present with depression'.

Task

If you are taking antidepressants, try this:

● *Calculate how long you have been on them (days, weeks, years).*

● *Now multiply by the dosage.*

That's how many pills you have popped. It may surprise you!

'SUNSHINE PILLS'

The 1990s saw the emergence of a new generation of antidepressants known as SSRIs (selective serotonin reuptake inhibitors), hailed, like all new-generation drugs, as 'without the harmful side effects of the previous generation'. SSRI prescription exploded. In Britain in 1997, around 6.5 million prescriptions were issued. By 2002 this had risen to 13.3 million. In the US, by 2003 more than 142 million prescriptions were dispensed, a staggering 45 per cent increase in three years. Antidepressants affect the brain's chemical messengers called neurotransmitters and may boost the level of serotonin. This slowly changes the brain's communication system – for good or ill. Some patients swear by them and find they help them through crises. But others have suffered serious harm.

Prozac (fluoxetine), the so-called 'sunshine drug' manufactured by Eli Lilly, was licensed in the US in 1988. Since then, although some sufferers have praised the drug for helping them, many cases have come to court in the US blaming Prozac for suicide and violence. Psychiatrist Dr David Healy, citing a wealth of statistical and medical evidence, writes: 'There is a long clinical tradition of recognizing anti-depressant-induced suicidality ... Companies have failed to report in full their clinical trial data on suicidal acts.'[2]

In early trials people who were *not* depressed had suicidal thoughts while on Seroxat, 'and the same is true of some people who are given SSRIs for conditions other than depression', MIND's Information Officer Dr Katherine Darton tells us. 'It is not always, or necessarily, the depression that makes people suicidal, as drug companies like to suggest. Some people have told us at MIND that they never felt like that before they started on the medication.'[3] Some patients have reported feeling violent rather than suicidal.

A study of 2,776 consecutive cases of DSH (deliberate self-harm) attending an accident and emergency department in 2000 found that occurrence 'was highest with fluoxetine (Prozac)'.[4] In one American court case, 76 research papers were cited to demonstrate that Prozac causes violence and suicide.[5] One patient, Joseph Wesbecker, a print worker from Louisville, shot eight colleagues, injured another 16 and then turned the gun on himself. Another, Bill Forsyth, a retired car rental company owner from California, took Prozac for 12 days and then stabbed his wife 15 times and impaled himself on the kitchen knife he had used. Ten days into his prescription course, Reginald Payne, a retired Cornish teacher, suffocated his wife and threw himself off a cliff.

Despite mega-dollar settlements out of court, Eli Lilly's position is always to blame the depression not the drug, but the risks of explosive tension and violent agitation (akathisia) had been recorded by the company since the drug's clinical trials in 1978. Plaintiffs claimed that Prozac had caused balanced individuals with mild depression to become suicidal killers.

OTHER SSRIs

In 2001 there was a landmark court ruling in the US in the case of Donald Schell, a retired oil-rig worker who had been taking the SSRI antidepressant Paxil for two days when he shot and killed his wife, daughter and granddaughter and then turned the gun on himself. The jury found that Paxil, made by GSK (GlaxoSmithKline), 'can cause some individuals to commit suicide and/or homicide' and awarded the surviving family members $8 million in damages.

In 2004, the US Food and Drug Administration asked the manufacturers of ten popular antidepressants to add suicide warning labels to their products. The drugs cited were:

Celexa	Paxil	Wellbutrin
Effexor	Prozac	Zoloft
Lexapro	Remeron	
Luvox	Serzone	

Long-suppressed research in the UK linking certain antidepressants with suicide among children and teenagers[6] had rung alarm bells in America. Of seven SSRI drugs under review by the Committee on Safety of Medicines – Celexa, Effexor, Lexapro, Luvox, Paxil, Prozac and Zoloft – four (Zoloft, Celexa, Paxil and Effexor) were found to increase the rate of self-harm. Official advice from the National Institute for Clinical Excellence (NICE) and the Medicines and Healthcare products Regulatory Agency (MHRA) in Britain is now to 'contraindicate' the use of SSRI antidepressants in patients under 18, apart from Prozac as a last resort combined with a talking treatment. Doubts have also been raised about the efficacy and effectiveness of Cipramil (citalopram) and Cipralex (escitalopram).[7]

SEROXAT

The best-selling antidepressant in the UK had been Seroxat (paroxetine), manufactured by GSK. The Committee on Safety of Medicines advises that patients should initially be given only 20 mg a day, but in 2003 it became clear that 17,000 patients had been started on higher doses and that Seroxat had been prescribed at unsafe levels since it was first licensed for use in the UK in 1990.[8] The drug has potentially disastrous side effects. Seroxat may raise the risk of suicide by as much as seven or eight times.[9]

The British drug regulatory body, the MHRA, is now investigating other reported problems with Seroxat – dubbed the 'anti-shyness pill' – such as anxiety, nausea, violent rages and suicidal thoughts. Janice Simmons of the Seroxat User Group expressed the anger of patients like herself: 'Prescribing of these drugs has become absolutely scandalous.'[10] NICE cautioned doctors in December 2004 to exercise more care in prescribing antidepressants. NICE advised that in cases of mild depression they should not be used at all. Andrew McCulloch of the Mental Health Foundation observed: 'The group of people who will benefit from these drugs is smaller than some GPs think.'[11] The situation is under review.

AND FINALLY – HOW WELL DO THEY WORK?

In response to a request under the (US) Freedom of Information Act from two psychologists, Thomas Moore and Irving Kirsch of the University of Connecticut, in

2002, a review was published of 47 studies used by the US Food and Drug Administration for approval of the six most commonly prescribed antidepressants between 1987 and 1999. These were (brand name first, generic name in brackets):

Zoloft (*sertraline*)	10.7 million prescriptions
Paxil (*paroxetine*)	10.49 million
Prozac (*fluoxetine*)	10 million
Celexa (*citalopram*)	5.29 million
Effexor (*venlafaxine*)	4.2 million
Serzone (*nefazodone*)	2.34 million

Overall the antidepressants performed slightly better than placebos, but in *more than half* the studies the drugs were no more effective than the sugar pills.[12]

So if you yourself have been prescribed antidepressants, take them out of the plastic pot or blister pack and look at them. Turn them over in your fingers. And then consider the following notes:

- Drugs for despair have been developed and tested using laboratory animals, pitiful analogues of human psychology.

- Antidepressant drugs are merely palliative. They may mask the effects of despair for a time, but they have a powerful attraction and you may develop a dependency on them in times of crisis, undermining your confidence to cope on your own.

- The British mental health charity MIND produces booklets on mood-altering drugs and how they have harmed some of those who use them. MIND say they can help some people to get through severe episodes but that patients should not take them without being fully informed of the risks.

- Patient groups like the Seroxat User Group, Beat the Benzos and Victims of Tranquillisers represent those who have suffered severe side effects from mood-altering drugs. Visit their websites and read their experiences.

Withdrawal

Side-effects – including suicidal thoughts – may increase during withdrawal and change of dose, but your GP can help you with this if you decide to go ahead. Withdrawal has to be sensibly managed – you can't just suddenly chuck the tablets in the toilet. But still, under medical supervision you can be gradually weaned off your mood-altering drugs once and for all.[13]

I hope when you have read this book you may feel that little sparkle inside that says *Go on – grow out of them*. Besides, unless you have recourse to a sensible strategy for dealing with it, despair tends to recur. The real cure lies not in your medicine cabinet, but in your brain:

- in knowledge
- in personal growth
- in challenges
- in realisation
- in discovering life skills
- in self-empowerment.

These will bring hope. Medical terminology will only bring medicines.

NOTES

1. Jeffrey Masson, *Against Therapy*. HarperCollins, 1997, p. 19.

2. David Healy, *Anti-depressants and Suicide*, Briefing Paper, 20 June 2003; David Healy, *The Anti-depressant Era*. Harvard University Press, 1999.

3. Katherine Darton, MIND Information Officer, 26 January 2010.

4. S. Donovan and R. Madeley, 'Deliberate self-harm and anti-depressant drugs', *British Journal of Psychiatry*, 177, 2000, pp. 551–6.

5. *Forsyth* v. *Eli Lilly*, in the US District Court of Hawaii, 5 January 1998.

6. 'FDA asks drug manufacturers to include suicide warnings', *Insight*, On the News, 22 March 2004.

7. Guardian.co.uk: *Health: Best Treatments* in partnership with the *British Medical Journal*, 'Depression in children', 3 December 2009.

8. MIND Press Release, 11 March 2004.

9. BBC2, *Horizon*, 'Pill poppers', 20 January 2010; Nigel Hawkes, 'Top-selling drug linked to increased suicide risk', *The Times* and *TimesOnline*, 22 August 2005.

10. Maxine Frith, 'Prozac nation, UK', *Independent*, 30 March 2004.

11. 'GPs get new anti-depressant rules', BBC News Online, 6 December 2004.

12. IMS Health, published in *USA Today*, 'Health and science', 7 July 2002; *Prevention and Treatment*, e-journal published by the American Psychological Association, 15 July 2002.

13. For the latest advice on withdrawal, see antidepressant expert Dr David Healy's protocol on http://www.seroxatusergroup.org.uk/David%20Healy%20Withdrawal%20Protocol%202009.pdf.

'Is it just me?'

You know, we might need to re-evaluate your condition. Why? Well, 'depression' is not simply *your* condition, is it? We can't account for it by saying there is *something wrong with you* personally, as though you were a lunatic or an emotional oddball. Literally millions of people are currently experiencing despair. Indeed, we are seeing what has been called a 'depression pandemic'.

THE DEPRESSION PANDEMIC

Consider these statistics:

- In the US among those under 30, 'major depression' has apparently doubled over the past 25 years, and depression is projected to become the second highest cause, after heart disease, of disability in the country.

- Ten million American children take antidepressants.

- An investigation by Columbia University discovered that since 1987 the number of Americans being treated for depression has risen from 1.8 million to 6.3 million.

- In Britain, according to government adviser on mental health Professor Richard Layhard, around 15% of the population suffers from depression or anxiety.

- The cost to the British economy is around £17 billion, or 1.5% of the gross domestic product.

- More than 6 million people in the UK regularly take antidepressants.

- The NHS bill for antidepressants shot up from £18 million in 1992 to £380 million in 2002, and today one in three GP patient appointments involves a patient reporting depression.

- In 2006 family doctors wrote out more than 730,000 prescriptions a week for happy pills, placing such pressure on the NHS drugs bill that medication for other conditions was being rationed.

- When Norwich Union Healthcare carried out a survey of GPs, eight out of ten doctors admitted that they were over-prescribing antidepressants and three-quarters said that they were prescribing more of these drugs than they were five years ago.

The excuse given was a 'dire shortage' of counsellors. Yet the counselling professions in the UK are booming and remain largely unregulated. The British Association for Counselling and Psychotherapy, by no means the only accrediting body, in 12 years increased its accredited membership by a staggering *804 per cent*. And even such exponential expansion in the number of counsellors has failed to halt the rise in depression.

TO HELL WITH THAT LOT – WHAT ABOUT ME?

What has all this got to do with you, sitting there feeling like Mr Death's PA? Well, as long as your 'depression' is treated as an illness afflicting *just you personally* – because you have a lot of problems, or because your problems are more serious than other people's problems, or because your serotonin or other brain chemicals are out of kilter, or because your grandmother had it and you are genetically predisposed – we are not seeing the bigger picture.

Depression is a pandemic, and if it is a pandemic, it must have an underlying cause. You don't get 'depression' from bugs. So the catalyst must lie elsewhere. I submit that the real reason for this global mushroom cloud of depression is this:

We have come to see our emotions – particularly negative emotions – as an inconvenience or an illness.

I therefore suggest that the most effective way to treat your 'depression' is to deal first of all with the ideology that has caused or contributed to it, and to show you how the current medicalising trend may have cast a pall of gloom over your emotional life. I say you didn't just jump into this bottomless pit. I say you were pushed.

Task

Find somebody you know over 60, preferably someone who lived through the last war. Ask them what happened to people who were depressed in the 1940s or during the Blitz. Were they given counselling or medication, or cocoa and Vera Lynn songs? What worked for them? How did they manage to survive?

EMOTIONS UNDER NEW MANAGEMENT

Attempts to manage unpleasant emotions – known collectively as 'stress management' – have led to the current fashion for soothing patients and chemically adapting their moods. Those who take 'stress management' drugs often do not realise the connection between tranquillisers and depression:

- Calming drugs are literally depressant drugs.

- Chemically they depress the central nervous system.

- Patients prescribed tranquillisers will often be given antidepressants to counter these 'depressing' effects.

- Other calm-down therapies, in so far as they tranquillise the user, may also sedate feelings.

Think about it: 'Anything for a quiet life.' If you have given your brain this instruction, what do you expect it to do? Yet because we are all busy and faced with lots of tasks and problems every day, *keeping calm* may have become your watchword, your unconscious aim in life. And who could blame you! Stress management exercises a very powerful influence over patient care and is on offer from most primary care trusts. Indeed, the theory of stress management currently determines public perception of emotional health, even though its provenance and scientific evidence are both highly questionable.

There are over 15 million websites on the Internet offering 'stress' advice, and the calm-down industry has increased exponentially. The stress industry has more practitioners than GPs or members of our armed forces, spreading what it calls 'stress awareness' and telling people to look out for signs and symptoms of a condition that has over 650 different (and opposite) definitions. Practitioners command huge fees but are not regulated by anyone but themselves.

Arguably, this vast industry has had a disabling effect on vulnerable people who now believe they are mentally abnormal whether they are or not, and many of them now fit the classification 'depressed'.

ARE MY FEELINGS SYMPTOMS?

When a person's emotional suffering is assessed from outside, innermost feelings may be viewed by mental health professionals in a technical or medical way. Being viewed or labelled as mentally ill makes us vulnerable, because our own interpretation of reality may no longer be accepted. Wishes and desires and fears and anxieties may be seen as symptoms requiring treatment. Yet feelings are important, real and deserving of respect.

They may also, under the circumstances, be perfectly normal. If you have lost a loved one, or your job, or your home, or your freedom, or all four (as one or two of my unemployed trainees had done) it would be pretty darn weird were you to feel chipper. There would really *be* something wrong with your brain.

All animals, from us to dogs and elephants, are frightened and angered by having precious things taken away, and mourn and grieve for what they have lost. This process is normal and natural. It is not a disease, and if we allow it to take its course, we grow and understand what has happened to us. But if we refuse to tolerate those bad feelings, behave as though we have a medical condition and then take drugs for it, we may well get stuck and not heal over. Despair then lingers. Nothing seems to shift it.

You are experiencing *the wet blanket effect*.

The wet blanket effect

You are in a box underneath a wet blanket. It is dark and dank in here. You are like a portrait of yourself with a black background. You have become unlucky. Your efforts are half-hearted and lifeless and so go pear-shaped. Everything looks bad and tastes bad. You can't explain to others the sort of wasteland that this makes of your life. You are at a standstill. Life goes on in the dim distance and seems not to have any relevance. You feel blank, yet scared. There is a bleak sense of foreboding that things will never get better, that there can never be a 'cure'.

You can in fact get out of this box. There *is* a cure, and the cure lies in the sufferer's own hands, though you will find it hard to believe this while despair is releasing its sedative substances into your brain.

The deadness makes it difficult to function, because the despairer does not care any more about life, or work, or relationships. There is no sense of being connected to others or to society. We are distanced and dissociated from everything that would normally be important, and from others, who fail to understand our state of mind. We are like dead people walking.

NOBODY UNDERSTANDS ME

Loved ones may look on in anguish and wonder whatever they can do to help. After a few attempts to get us to 'cheer up' (or pull ourselves together), they may become exasperated by their own impotence, and then impatient with the 'patient'. This in turn disinclines the sufferer from bothering anybody about that inner wasteland. We may simply keep silent or speak in monosyllables or become morose with others, increasing the communication gulf. Despair is a desperately lonely complaint.

So in the next chapter we shall be getting insights from others who have been through what you are going through, people who have been able to express what it is really like, people who have *understood*. The fact that they were all geniuses should help: they may even give you back your sense of kinship with mankind. As Christine sings to the *Phantom of the Opera*, buried in the bowels of the theatre and frightened to come out because he is a touch disfigured:

> *Pitiful creature of darkness:*
> *What kind of life have you known?*
> *God give me courage to show you*
> *You are not alone.*

When words fail you

Knowing that there are millions of other people suffering from depression may not help you personally. One laboratory animal can only feel its own pain: it doesn't get any comfort from statistics on all the others. Yet a sense of kinship with people who have gone through the hell of despair and expressed it, and worked through it and triumphed over it, could provide a lifeline to you.

But *who has been there*? Not your average therapist or mental health expert, certainly. Not your psychological or psychiatric theorist and thankfully not most of your inner circle either ('thankfully' because you wouldn't wish this on them). But some of our greatest writers, poets, composers and painters *have* been there. They had an intimate knowledge of personal despair – yet they fought it, vanquished it, used it to drive and enrich their work. When you choose your heroes, consider the courage of people who have done this.

Despair vanquished: the case of Ludwig van Beethoven

Beethoven reached a crisis of misery and loneliness when he realised he had lost his hearing and that there was no cure. It was the worst thing that could possibly happen to a composer who depended on sound for his inspiration. He was far beyond tears. He thought very carefully of committing suicide and wrote a letter intended for his family telling them in a dignified way how he had failed and intended to give it all up. Yet Beethoven stayed his hand, and went on to write the most triumphant music of his or any life.

Despair vanquished: the case of Etty Hillesum

You may never have heard of Etty, who like Anne Frank kept a diary during the war and lived in Amsterdam. Like Anne she was Jewish and eventually killed by the Nazis. But Etty was 27, fully aware of what was going on, and her diary shows her transformation from utter despair and terror to inspiration and courage. The entry for Thursday, 10 November 1941 reads: 'Mortal fear in every fibre. Complete collapse. Lack of self-confidence. Aversion. Panic.' Yet by 1942 she was writing: 'I am a happy person and I hold life dear indeed ... I know just as long as one small street is left to us, the whole firmament still stretches far above it. I've died a thousand deaths in a thousand concentration camps ... and yet I find life beautiful and meaningful. From minute to minute.'[1]

Despair vanquished: the case of Winston Churchill

Churchill suffered from terrible bouts of apathy and despair. He called it his 'black dog'. He took to painting not terribly good pictures, building brick walls in his garden and voracious reading to win back his ferocious fighting spirit. Because his 'lion-hearted nation' knew that he had done this, they were willing to trust his leadership during the Blitz when their world seemed very dark indeed. Churchill's wartime speeches are among the most famous calls to courage ever recorded, and they galvanised a nation.

SCIENTISTS 'DISCOVER' LITERATURE

One branch of the arts that may be especially useful to you when you are beginning your fightback against despair is literature. Reading is now officially recognised as beneficial to our emotions. If you have never read a classic novel or a powerful poem, you have missed the door to an Aladdin's cave, one that may give you back your sense of wonder and purpose. There's growing scientific evidence that enjoying the great works of fiction and verse can make us feel and function better. Mankind has known about this link for centuries – we just haven't always exploited it.

In January 2009 a Wellcome Collection event in London, promoted jointly by the UK's Reader Organisation and the medical journal *The Lancet*, highlighted the work of international scientists and doctors on the health-giving effects of literature. 'The Reading Cure' publicised new evidence linking reading with healthful brain changes that promote creativity, empathy and self-belief. This was not just another boffin conference. It may affect the way British doctors treat depression in the future. Professor Louis Appleby, NHS Director of Mental Health, said that this was 'exactly the kind of work we at the Department of Health want to develop over the next ten years.'

HOW LITERATURE 'WORKS'

Oh, literature – ho hum, you may think if you have never gone there. Why the fuss? Well, in a classic work of fiction, the reader communes not only with the writer but with characters on their emotional adventures, experiencing and understanding the effects on them. Reading is very different from watching characters in a television series. You are alone with the writer, who is a wordsmith with special insight into language that invokes powerful emotions and ideas. That language is specialised and highly concentrated. In a poem this is signalled by short lines on the page.

In a classic novel you go through what the characters go through, and often there is a hero or heroine whose journey you share. Very important is that your experience with them is resolved and complete – you are not left hanging in the air at the finish, as you so often are with television series and soaps. The writer makes vivid what the characters are thinking and feeling, and the ending makes sense of the whole.

A great novel or poem can throw light on even the most soul-desiccating and turbulent human emotions – including despair itself. Because the words reach into your soul, literature does what television cannot. It stays with you, and the words linger. They have impact. They give you goosebumps. They can make you laugh, or weep with joy. This is why, in scientific experiments monitoring the brains of people reading classic novels, ripples of activation and pleasure are detected by the equipment.

Task 1: A story that grabs you

Even if you've never done so before, I want you to pay a visit to my 'church'. There's one in every town. It's not an ordinary church but a Book Church, otherwise known as your local library. Go in and have a look round: shelves full of these strange collections of bound pages, spines facing outwards. Not technological, yet they tower above you. Some of them were written hundreds of years ago. Some weigh a ton.

Sense the atmosphere. Libraries are quiet, because most people respect the thousands of books that are housed here and speak in a whisper. In one section there are computers, but you won't be going on those. What you are about to do can't be experienced on a computer, or on the Internet. You have to be in this place to get the 'feel' for it.

I want you to walk over to the shelves marked FICTION, and without paying particular attention to the spines, or the authors' names or titles, take down a book and open it in the middle. Read a paragraph or two. Put the book back on the shelf and repeat this three times so that you have looked inside four books. This is exactly how generations of children have discovered the joys of reading for the first time. You still see adults doing it in bookshops, on stations and at the airport. Dip in and look at the words till you find the ones you want.

One of those books will catch your attention, because of the language, or the dialogue, or the story. Look at the spine and remember the title, and the name of the author. You can even check it out for free if you like. Take it home and find out what happens.

THE 'BLUE DEVILS'

Famous writers achieve their fame because they entertain us with their imaginative ideas, and because they put into words what we all feel. One literary genius who famously suffered from despair was the so-called Northampton Peasant Poet John Clare, who was stricken by the 'blue devils' yet produced over ten thousand pages of manuscript, an outpouring of passionate observation of nature, both in poetry and prose, the sheer volume and immediacy of which is unrivalled anywhere in English literature. He wrote:

> *I am – yet what I am – who cares, or knows?*
> *My friends forsake me like a memory lost;*
> *I am the self-consumer of my woes:*
> *They rise and vanish, an oblivious host*
> *Like shadows in love's frenzied stifled throes*
> *And yet I am; I live, like vapours tossed*
> *Into the nothingness of scorn and noise,*
> *Into the living sea of waking dreams,*
> *Where there is neither sense of life nor joys,*
> *But the vast shipwreck of my life's esteem,*
> *And all that's dear, e'en those I love the best*
> *Are strange – nay, they are stranger than the rest ...*

EXERCISE

- Look at John Clare's words. He wrote them when he was consigned to a mental asylum and had lost everything. He keeps saying, again and again, *I am*. Why?

- Some of the words are 'archaic' – like 'e'en' and 'nay', but most of them convey exactly the same sense to us as they would have done to Clare 150 years ago.

- They are stark. They repeat the same thought, and they are insistent and driven ('into the nothingness ... into the living sea'). Is the writer saying things in different ways because he hopes finally to be understood in one of them? Or is he trying to make sense of very painful ideas and feelings that threaten to overwhelm him?

- Some expressions are unfamiliar to us, like 'love's frenzied throes'. What does he mean by that?

- Look at the style. Why are the words written in short lines on the page? If you wrote them out like prose, as though they were a story in a newspaper, would they seem like ordinary everyday language to you? If not, why not?

- Why do poets often use rhythm and rhyme? Do the words sound like an incantation or a song? Is there any other reason?

- Poets have talked about 'the language of the heart', meaning words that spring from the imagination rather than analytical intelligence. Is this 'the language of the heart'?

Task 2: Finding the right words

While you are in the Book Church, go over to the section marked POETRY. If you can't find it ask at the desk. There is one. Try to wipe the look of embarrassment off your face because the word 'poetry' is not macho or modern, and because you may associate it with old-fashioned birthday cards, or doggerel written by talentless twits in love.

Real poetry is simply this: very powerful condensed language. The German word for poetry is Gedichte, *which actually means 'condensation' or 'concentration'. The words are locked together very tight. The poet Samuel Taylor Coleridge said that in a truly great poem, to change just one of the words would wreck the whole, so carefully have they been chosen. A lot of the words carry more than one meaning, so that when you read them the first time, you may only pick up on one. Read again, and you'll notice more.*

Most poems are about emotions. Perhaps yours. William Wordsworth said that poetry was 'powerful feelings recollected in tranquillity'. Open one of the books and run your eyes down the verses. Find one that holds you. Then look at the title, and the name of the poet. That's it. You can go home now. But remember the Book Church and come back here again!

NOTE

1. Etty Hillesum, *Etty, a Diary 1941–43.* Jonathan Cape, 1983.

The 'born loser'

MINDSETS OF DOOM

Anyone knows what 'feeling a bit down' is like. Such sadness is generally short-lived: low spirits, a bad mood. Life is full of ups and downs and these are the downs. But when the downs become so long-lasting and so severe that we are permanently trapped in a dark cloud, we are experiencing despair. Despairers may adopt the following mental strategies:

- Apathy – *I can't be bothered.*

- Resignation – *I give up, I give in, I submit to anything.*

- Hopelessness – *I don't expect anything will come of this – it's all futile.*

- Stoicism – *I never get excited about anything: it all rolls over me.*

- Effort thrift – *If I never try, I reckon I can't fail.*

- Cynicism – *I can knock anything down with my joyless quips.*

These are all controlling mindsets. They are also destructive mindsets. They place controls on mental energy and emotion in order to avoid pain and effort. They limit the amount of belief and faith we are prepared to give to anything, or anyone. They are mean and miserly with our feelings, yet the whole effect is to render us emotionally bankrupt.

These mindsets are often the recourse of people who believe they are somehow *unfortunate*, *doomed* or *unlucky*. Born losers may act tough, or they may wallow in self-pity, but deep down they feel the cards are stacked against them, that life is utterly unfair. And the trouble is they are generally proven right. Such mindsets work like self-fulfilling prophesies, because if you think like a loser, you tend to behave like a loser and you look like a loser in the mirror and to other people. Reality reflects back what we think and believe, like this:

nothing goes out ↔ nothing comes in

nothing ventured ↔ nothing gained

no dream or goal ↔ no motivation

no effort ↔ no success

no change ↔ no improvement

DEAF TO ALL ENTREATIES

When I worked as a 'scary Mary' Restart trainer, long-term unemployed people used to come on my courses with a negative mindset. A lot of them seemed *permanently fed up*. For these demoralised souls, nothing had ever gone right, and nothing would ever go right. If you asked them what's the matter, the conversation generally went something like this:

Talking to the 'born loser' (male)

'What's up?'

'Don't ask.'

'I am asking.'

'Oh, our house was burgled and I lost my computer.'

'Don't worry – claim it on the insurance.'

'I haven't got any Insurance.'

'Why not?'

'I can't afford it.'

'Why not?'

'I'm out of work.'

'Why can't you find work?'

'I'm too old' or 'I'm not qualified' or 'I'm not good at interviews' or 'I can't get up in the mornings' or 'I'm not confident with other people.'

'Why not?'

At this point you may as well give up, because you won't get anywhere – at least not like this. The person you are talking to has inwardly resigned himself to misfortune on a permanent basis. He doesn't have any hope, or resources, or prospects. He feels like a loser, and therefore behaves like a loser, with fairly predictable results. He believes he is doomed to bad luck and unhappiness and that all his efforts will prove futile.

Another example is the girl who behaves as though she doesn't like boys. It turns out that she doesn't like her appearance either. You try talking to her.

> **Talking to the 'born loser' (female)**
> *'Why don't you like boys?'*
> *'They don't like me.'*
> *'What makes you think that?'*
> *(Shrug.) 'Dunno.'*
> *'What makes you think they don't like you?'*
> *'They don't talk to me.'*
> *'Do you talk to them?'*
> *'No.'*
> *'Why not?'*
> *'They don't like me.'*

This girl has made up her mind that she is destined for a life alone. Even if you introduce her to a nice young man and he asks her out, she will very likely bite his head off.

It is very difficult to reason with a 'born loser'. Even if they go into therapy, the notion that they are somehow destined to be at the bottom of the heap is very hard to shift. As they see it, life is a vicious circle, and very vicious towards them, no matter what they do. Even if somebody tries to help them, it must be because of pity or some ulterior motive. Born losers will put up barrier after barrier to helpful suggestions from friends, family, colleagues, counsellors. The born loser has the power to bring other people down, like a drowning man grabbing at his rescuer. Eventually others lose patience and begin to avoid such 'saddoes' altogether – yet another self-fulfilling prophesy confirmed. And when all else fails, the born loser has one final mental strategy up his sleeve. It is this:

● Helplessness – *Someone must take pity on me. I can't manage.*

Unfortunately that doesn't usually work either. It simply annoys people.

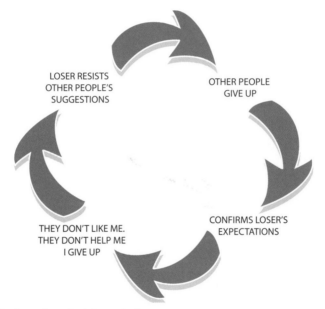

Fig. 1 *The born loser's vicious circle.*

Clearly, we need to get to the bottom of this psychological mystery of what *makes* born losers. Those who adopt destructive mindsets become trapped in their circular thinking like hamsters in a wheel. When they have the chance to interact with the world, they grit their teeth and dig their heels in. They say 'no' a lot. They behave like victims rather than survivors. It ruins their lives and wrecks their chances, yet they can't stop doing it, and on the surface it *doesn't make sense.* Strangely, there is a centuries-old philosophy that underpins this self-defeating behaviour.

THE 'GLOOM AND DOOM' MERCHANTS

For generations in Western culture, there has been a link between *gloom* and *doom* – between simply feeling downcast over current circumstances and feeling that one is *destined to be a loser*. In the past, for example in Calvinist and Puritan thinking, hopelessness and depression were not seen as mood disorders or diseases of the mind in the way they are today. A tendency to melancholia was thought to be based on one's personal balance of 'humours' in the body (air, fire, water and earth). But despair itself   that disabling black hopelessness that destroys all effort and will – was looked upon as a spiritual state. It was considered 'sinful' and a sign that God must have turned His face away from the sufferer, who was therefore lacking in 'grace' – that magic cloud of love, luck and positive energy that you get when someone upstairs likes you.

For the Puritans, there was a widely accepted analogy between personal despair and economic ruin, and not just because debtors' prisons like Sponge Row were full of people in abject despair. The Puritans believed in hard work. They didn't spend their money in conspicuous consumption like the Catholics of the period. They were thrifty, and a lot of them were shopkeepers and middle-class business folk. They saved their money and kept careful accounts and diaries. To these people, evidence of failure to build up a respectable store of wealth and success by hard work in this life – in other words, bankruptcy, destitution or reliance on illegitimate trade like thieving or harlotry – were taken as a sign that the ruined person was predestined for one thing: *to go to Hell*. One's fortune *prefigured* one's eventual Fortune. 'The rich man in his castle, the poor man at his gate' – it was all providential.

THE PURITANS AND THE 'CASTAWAY'

Unlike the *non*-despairing, hardworking and frugal middle-class Puritans who were evidently going to be saved, the poor man in despair was known as a 'castaway'. Bankrupts could be sent to Newgate, and then literally 'cast' or hanged. Dr Johnson in his famous dictionary defines the castaway as 'one cast away from the ship of the Elect' (meaning the saved). The terrible predicament of this blighted soul meant that he kept up his anxious shadow-boxing all his life, miserably struggling on, as much from fear of extinction as anything else.

John Bunyan was almost overwhelmed with anxiety at the thought of being a castaway. In Pilgrim's Progress, *Despair is a terrifying monster, and Christian has to get away from it and out of the Slough of Despond by his courage and effort. He succeeds in the end.*

John Milton, another Puritan writer, explored the predicament of the very first 'Castaway', Satan, in his epic Paradise Lost. *Throughout the poem Milton's Devil is trying to 'build a heaven in hell's despair'. Although Milton was a devoutly religious man and loved God, his depiction of the Devil somehow emerges as a glorious character, a fallen angel doomed to perpetual torment but refusing to give up. Milton was a political activist. He reached out almost to grasp his utopia, only to be thrown in prison by his opponents, bereaved of two successive wives and a son, struck blind and robbed of all his hopes. What he wrote came from his heart, and it was about the grandeur of fighting despair. If you read the poem, he gives his Devil all the best lines.*

DEFYING 'FATE': DANIEL DEFOE

The Puritan attitude to despairers, financial failures and 'castaways' also appalled our 'first novelist' Daniel Defoe, who although he was a Puritan, felt that such a judgement on a living person was unjust and repugnant. Defoe, himself a bankrupt, suffered from bouts of dark despair and was keenly interested in the predicament of the 'castaway' (including the first Castaway in his own very sympathetic *History of the Devil*). In *Journal of the Plague Year* Defoe examined despair from a journalistic viewpoint, looking at the bravery, audacity and pragmatism of ordinary people surrounded by infection and death – a doom *they* believed was deliberately sent by God. The *Journal* shows Defoe's contempt for the Calvinist 'unalterable destiny'.

Several of his classic novels deal with characters faced with hopeless ruin but who eventually triumph over their fate. The most famous of these was the tale of his castaway *Robinson Crusoe*.

Robinson Crusoe is shipwrecked and stranded on an island that he actually names 'Despair'. Never intended to be a children's book, *Crusoe* starts from the basis of bleak ruin and hopelessness. This is the spiritual condition on which Crusoe has to 'go to work' and from which he hopes by his efforts to be delivered. If the present-day 'born loser' were to sit down and read *Robinson Crusoe* as an allegory about self-redemption, its meaning will become patently clear. The book has the power seriously to raise your spirits. Daniel Defoe was one bankrupt despairer who rose like a phoenix.

Experiencing the great arts classics, whether these are cinematic, musical or literary, enhances the soul, especially the lost soul. Reading the masterpieces of those who have shared your experiences can speak to you with an insight and immediacy you won't find in a doctor's waiting room or a therapist's surgery or from swallowing prescription (and non-prescription) chemicals.

Besides, present-day despairers are not like the Puritans with their foreboding fear of predestination. We are a bit more enlightened now and realise that gloom doesn't *have* to turn into doom at all. If it seems that way, this is often because of a temptation to generalise bad feelings or bad luck and to attribute them to some outside source. Psychologists call this having 'an exterior locus of control' – giving power away to some other person or force that decides what becomes of us.

'Castaway' behaviour

People who are prone to helplessness and apathy have often 'taken their hands off the steering wheel' because they believe 'others' or some 'other force' controls their destiny. They wait in vain for these 'others' or 'the fates' to smile upon them. They tend to be superstitious. They have 'lucky' numbers and spend their money on lottery tickets hoping to be 'rescued in the end'. If you keep leaving your fate to chance like this, you are sitting in your car waiting for an accident to happen.

Just drive!

Nobody is really a born loser. We convince ourselves that we are because of traditional ideas and beliefs that do not fit our case any more. You may feel bad now, but by your assertive actions and problem-solving skills you are not going to feel half so bad tomorrow. Read on, and find out how to become, not a castaway, but the captain of your fate.

EXERCISE

Think of a book or a movie that you have seen that 'raised your spirits'. (You may need to refresh your memory by reading or seeing it again.)

1 How did it work its magic on your feelings?

2 Could it have worked if the hero (or heroine) had not gone through a terrible ordeal in the first place?

3 Was there a critical point at which the hero decided to fight?

4 Were you allowed to think all his efforts might fail? If so, why?

5 What do we actually mean by 'raising your spirits'?

6 Does it have to happen by chance, or is it possible to do it deliberately?

7 What action would you take if you had to raise a team's spirits, or an army's, or a nation's (for example during a war)?

8 Write yourself a pep talk. You can do it!

Mental illness labels

Despair is one of the worst kinds of human anguish, the equal of even the severest physical pain. When a man cannot be bothered to get out of bed and walk over to the sink to clean his teeth because there seems no point to it, or when a woman keeps the curtains drawn and hides indoors because she can no longer face the world, talking about the validity or harm of mental illness classifications may not seem that important.

But they *are* important. Having been given a 'condition' can have an impressive effect on your mind and body. It can cause a cascade of symptoms, like this:

It starts by making you feel abnormal.

This makes you worry about your health.

Then if your label is psychological it makes you anxious about your sanity.

This anxiety in turn can cause physiological changes: over-alertness, raised blood pressure, palpitations, sweating, sleeplessness.

Suddenly you don't just feel bad and have all the original problems that upset you in the first place.

Now you have an illness as well!

In the scientific literature this has become known as the *nocebo* effect.[1] Unlike the *placebo* effect, in which positive beliefs about even sugar pills can aid recovery, the nocebo effect refers to negative and morbid beliefs that *undermine* recovery and make the patient worse. They may even prove fatal.

THE 'I NEED A SYNDROME' SYNDROME

Life can be very cruel. It can be outrageously unfair. We all get hurt and disappointed and we all suffer life's 'slings and arrows'. But we don't all suffer from 'depression'. So does depression *only* strike those who have suffered the highest number of bad events or the most severe misfortunes? The research suggests not. The survivors of an air crash, for example, may actually be more positive and well-balanced than they were before.[2] The majority of people exposed to distressing experiences do not go on to develop mental illness. If they did, we should all be mentally ill.

In my own experience, 'depression' and severe experiences do not necessarily happen to the same people. Some individuals I know have gone through the most horrendous ordeals and yet maintain a positive outlook.[3] Yet others who have suffered relatively minor misfortunes have turned away from life, sunk into inertia and 'given up'. As I am known as a Heartless Bitch, please don't take my word for this. You can test the theory yourself.

Objectivity test

Without telling anybody or showing them the list you are about to make, write down the names of people you know well. Next to each name, write down bad things that you know have happened to them in the past. For every terrible life event, give them one point. Then add up their scores (be honest and don't manipulate on the basis of your personal preferences). Now, look at the high scores. Are all of those people 'depressed'? If not, why not? Are all of the depressed people you know high scorers? If not, why not?

Many people *believe* they suffer from 'depression' or 'clinical depression' simply because they are grieving over one of life's maulings, don't know what to do to feel better and think it might help if they had a label for their bad feelings. The label acts like a baby's dummy or Linus's security blanket – he sucks his thumb and holds it to his ear in times of trouble, though it doesn't actually serve any useful purpose. We all use the term 'depression' willy-nilly, and as the media constantly spice up their health pages and programmes with it, the word becomes difficult to avoid. But it is important to remember that this label is not a cure, and that it may demoralise you.

Give your psyche a bad name and you may get stuck with it.

Why do some of us like to be labelled? Why do people willingly undergo diagnosis or self-diagnosis? Because it confers certain advantages:

1 The label becomes a kind of lucky talisman to ward off the unknown.

2 It places the scary disorder within certain parameters.

3 It ring-fences the condition so that it doesn't get completely out of hand.

4 It suggests science is 'on your case'.

5 It suggests that scientists and psychologists 'understand' you.

6 It suggests that there is a medical cure.

You may think: 'Oh, somebody has nailed down what's wrong with me. They know all about it. Science is onto this. They'll be able to cure me now!' But this is mere superstition. Mental illness diagnoses don't actually help recovery. They don't even accurately identify the problem. In all likelihood, they make sufferers feel worse, especially if they are accompanied by reliance on mood-altering chemicals that further erode their sense of independence and self-esteem. People generally do not feel good about having a 'mental complaint' or having to alter their minds by pushing drugs in their faces.

Once patients are officially labelled 'depressed' – or, heaven forbid, 'clinically depressed' – it tends to be written in invisible ink across their foreheads and may sap what little energy they had left to get off their bottoms and set about changing their outlook on life. Some of them, in an age seemingly obsessed with the milder forms of mental illness, then wear their label like a badge of honour and mention it at every opportunity. The more unscrupulous ones use it to get time off work, claim benefits and curry favour with friends. Celebrities seem not at all bashful about their depressive disorders. They even appear on chat shows to discuss their symptoms and syndromes, and bore into them in ghosted autobiographies. Publishers call these 'misery memoirs' and a lot of these 'sorry ass' books are best-sellers.

Of course it is our moral duty as a society to care for and protect the genuinely mentally ill. But in the current stress management age, our emotional lives are routinely managed and medicalised. Classifying millions of people with impressive-sounding psychological 'conditions' and then applying mental illness labels to their feelings can harm them. Not only may they be trapped in a diagnostic prison and fall victim to a syndrome that they are supposed to have and never get out. The situation is worse than that.

Doctor, doctor – my label's fallen off

In November 2008 BBC TV's flagship science programme Horizon *conducted a two-week experiment in which a panel of mental health 'experts' tried to identify six disorders – schizophrenia, social anxiety, eating disorder (either bulimia or anorexia nervosa), depression, bi-polar disorder and obsessive compulsive disorder – among ten volunteers after watching them perform a series of challenges. Five volunteers had been assessed as 'normal' and five were suffering from one of the named conditions. The three experts, Professor Richard Bentall, psychologist Ian Hulatt and Dr Michael First, were able to match just two conditions to their sufferers. They landed several people with conditions they did not possess.*

Eminent critics like Jeffrey Masson[4] and Peter Breggin[5] say mental illness labels need to be viewed with extreme caution, and Masson, himself a former psychoanalyst and custodian of Freud's papers, says they are more akin to intellectual flag-waving than useful tools in diagnosis.

WOUNDING THE MIND

Another term commonly applied to depressed people is that they were *traumatised* by some terrible experience at some time in their lives, and this is why they are now 'clinically depressed'. Having been 'traumatised', of course, there is little hope for them.

- They will have to be wrapped in cotton wool from now on.

- Their minds are like mangled cars about to be towed away to the breakers after a smash.

- Only years of expensive counselling or psychotherapy can possibly restore their mutilated psyches.

- They will need all the drugs they can get.

- They needn't think of going back to work, even supposing they were thinking of it.

- They should avoid any excitement. They could be kicked to death by butterflies, so fragile is their sanity now.

And so on – you get my drift. *Traumatised.* We hear it all the time – schoolchildren have seen an accident in the playground and are therefore 'traumatised'. A woman has been attacked in the street and is 'traumatised'. Bank staff who were on duty during a raid have all been 'traumatised'. Viewers can apparently even be 'traumatised' by watching a particularly challenging episode of *EastEnders*.

People in Haiti must surely have been 'traumatised' by the devastating earthquake that struck their poverty-stricken state at the beginning of 2010. Yet some of those pulled out of the rubble in Port-au-Prince after days without food or water were actually smiling and talking normally. Incredibly, one woman was cheerfully *singing*. News cameras filmed her being driven away in the front passenger seat of a four-by-four, her features as casual and composed as someone being picked up after work. How could this be? Surely she should be *devastated* (another very popular media disaster word). She must be *pretending* to be OK. She will surely *break down later*.

PROBLEMS WITH 'PTSD'

In the West, the diagnosis of Post Traumatic Stress Disorder, or PTSD, has come under attack from a variety of mental health experts on the grounds that it may be misleading, unscientific and potentially disabling to the victim.[6] The diagnosis has arisen because of an influential theory – that the *mind can be wounded*. This theory may in fact be wrong.

The word 'trauma', which has slipped into the vernacular during any discussion on disaster victims, is Greek for 'injury'. Saying that the *psyche* (more Greek) has been injured when it has no corporeal form is a poetic and powerful metaphor. It helps others who have not shared a terrible experience to understand the intensity of mental suffering involved, and to treat the sufferer with compassion and respect. But whether it is literally true that the psyche can be injured is a very moot point. As I explained in the relevant analysis in my book on 'stress':

> To describe someone as 'traumatised' presupposes that painful emotions and experiences are wounds or abrasions in need of medical treatment; that they are not normal to life; that human beings cannot absorb and respond to them successfully; that they cannot recover, learn and grow. Survivors who are medically labelled in this way may end up not survivors at all, but 'victims', thinking that they are 'psychologically scarred' or 'emotionally crippled', or that they are owed compensation, or that some

person or authority must rectify whatever misery and fear they may have felt.[7]

Dr James Thompson, one of the first British psychiatrists to popularise the PTSD diagnosis in the UK, says that it has become a safety blanket that protects people from worrying questions about their competence in a crisis. He says:

> Knowledge of PTSD and its symptoms is now so widespread – I blame myself ... There is pressure from people who are stressed and agitated: 'Say I am traumatized – I fit the disorder.' The motive is clear: which description would you prefer about yourself: 'He collapsed because of the *extreme stress* placed upon him', or 'He collapsed because he is a weak, fragile individual who could not cope with life'?[8]

'Suffering from PTSD' would absolve this person from responsibility for not coping, whereas just being 'fragile' would not.

Post-incident debriefing can make you worse

The cluster of reactions that have come to be called 'PTSD' may be distressing, painful and frightening. But if they happen to be the means whereby the brain gradually comes to terms with distressing events (flashbacks, for example, may be prompts to think about a memory that is deliberately being avoided), then this process may be prolonged by ill-advised interventions like 'post-incident debriefing' that require the survivor to revisit his feelings again and again. Some very well conducted studies have shown that these medical interventions make the victim worse, not better.[9] Indeed, if therapy is forced on the victim in the immediate aftermath, it may have a nocebo effect. Medical intervention after a disaster may create in the mind of the survivor the idea that his or her reactions are abnormal and a sign of mental illness, and that he or she is therefore mentally ill. Such fears can predispose the sufferer to pessimism, anxiety, helplessness and disease.

So if you have been 'diagnosed', don't just sit there and succumb. Your brain has literally billions of neurons, and most of them aren't being used (most of them have *never* been used). Scientists know that the brain's spare storage capacity is prodigious, and it has seemingly miraculous untapped powers of recovery just lying there, waiting to help you survive and grow, waiting for you to say, *Blast all this. I'm going to get better.*

The 'nocebo effect' routed

In J. R. R. Tolkien's Lord of the Rings, *King Théodon sits staring and frozen to his throne, unable to get his act together for the coming war because his sinister adviser Grimer Wormtongue keeps whispering that he is weak and hopeless. When the wizard Gandalf kicks Grimer out of the palace, the King resumes his heroic power.*

Just remember the lady who sang in Port-au-Prince. Her hair may have been sticking out and her face may have been covered in cement dust, but her human spirit was alive and well, thank you very much, doctor.

NOTES

1. See, for example, Helen Pilcher, 'The science of voodoo: when the mind attacks the body', *New Scientist*, 2708, 13 May 2009.

2. Angela Patmore, *The Truth About Stress*. Grove Atlantic, 2006, pp. 274–5.

3. *The Truth About Stress*, pp. 6–7.

4. Jeffery Masson, *Against Therapy*, foreword Dorothy Rowe. Collins, 1989.

5. Peter Breggin, *Toxic Psychiatry*. St Martin's Press, 1991. Peter R. Breggin MD has been called 'the conscience of psychiatry' for his efforts to reform the mental health field. He has written a number of books on caring psychotherapeutic approaches and the escalating overuse of psychiatric medications, oppressive diagnosing and drugging of children, involuntary treatment, electroshock and lobotomy.

6. See, for example, *The Truth About Stress*, pp. 249–75.

7. *The Truth About Stress*, p. 259.

8. Quoted in Kevin Toolis, 'Shock tactics', *Guardian Weekend*, 13 November 1999.

9. See, for example, J. Bisson, P. Jenkins *et al.*, 'Randomised controlled trial of psychological debriefing for victims of acute burn trauma', *British Journal of Psychiatry*, 171, 1997, pp. 78–81; R. A. Mayou, A. Ehlers and M. Hobbs, 'Psychological debriefing for road traffic accident victims: three-year follow-up of a randomised controlled trial', *British Journal of Psychiatry*, 176, 2000, pp. 589–93.

The harm of calm

That's right – lie there in your herbal 'de-stressing' bath. Have a good soak. Play with your rubber duck if you like – I've nothing against relaxation. *So long as you realise that, when you get out of that extremely relaxing bath, you will have exactly the same set of problems as you did when you got into it.*

Just being calm doesn't solve problems. What it *can* do is to sooth you into thinking things aren't really that urgent or important, when in fact they may *be* that urgent and important. Self-sedation can enable people who are already prone to helplessness and problem-avoidance and who face serious challenges requiring urgent action to go bumbling on for a bit longer without doing anything to help themselves – during which time their problems may very well have ballooned out of control. No wonder they are also depressed.

Yet people *behave* like this because they have been told to avoid something called 'stress'. The National Health Service spends millions of pounds it can ill afford on drugs intended to alleviate the said 'stress'. We chemically cosh our children and our old folk as well as ourselves to achieve the optimum state of nation sedation. 'Anything for a quiet life' has become our watchword.

THE 'STRESS' BUSINESS

So-called 'stress management' experts do not like me. A lot of people who make a handsome living from 'stress' expertise and 'stress' remedies would like to see me at the bottom of a pond. This is because I have exposed the flaws in their so-called scientific evidence and questioned the efficacy and effectiveness of their techniques. My book *The Truth About Stress* offers 400 pages of evidence plus 40 pages of scientific references to show that the unregulated 'stress' industry – with its 15 million websites and its millions of practitioners, some of them completely unqualified and spouting pseudo-scientific rubbish – is harming people and making them depressed.

For a start the whole stress business, even on its own terms, has failed. The more the industry plies its trade and enlarges its membership base (growing at a rate of 804% in 12 years) the more the 'stress' statistics skyrocket. Practitioners can't even tell us under the Trade Descriptions Act what they are managing. Plus they haven't managed it. During the year I spent typing up my book, according to the Health and Safety Executive (HSE) yet another 245,000 people in the UK 'became aware' that they were suffering from 'stress'.

What are stress sufferers suffering from?

BBC TV filmed me a while back unfurling a list of over 650 different definitions on Paddington station, with commuters coming over and adding more. Meanings come from the scientific literature, from health authorities, from stress management persons and sufferers. Many are opposites. The HSE, for instance, use the s-word to mean a type of response (a 'natural reaction'). Yet some scientists who specialise in the field like Professor Angela Clow use it to mean a type of stimulus (she talks about 'responses to stress' and cortisole as 'a biomarker of stress'). Professor Stafford Lightman, another authority, uses it to mean both. He says: 'We've been involved in an intensive programme to design a pill which can counter the effects of stress. And the way to do this is to block the first chemical made by the hypothalamus in the brain which actually controls the whole of the stress response.'[1] So now we can have the same word used to mean two opposites in the same explanation from one authority. In any other field of science this would not be tolerated. Even the éminence grise of 'stress' expertise, Professor Cary Cooper, has said on numerous occasions that stress is when something: 'Stress occurs when pressure exceeds your perceived ability to cope.' But this is not a definition. The definition of 'cat' is not 'when something is furry'.

Then there are the lay definitions. These include many very different feelings. Other 'meanings' refer to external problems, like overwork, not enough work, no work, sitting still in traffic, rushing about, being bullied, having domestic troubles. Finally 'stress' can mean an impressive variety of physiological mechanisms: fight-or-flight, heart rate, hormonal secretions during any or all of the above, and so on. All real, all different, all being medicalised and turned into a disease.

The stress industry's mantra is this:

Being calm is normal and the key to a healthy life.

This is untrue, but you need to remember that the stress industry *sells* calm.

Calming methods marketed as 'stress management'

Meditation techniques	Hypnosis
Deep breathing	T'ai chi/martial arts
Visualisation	Postural relaxation
Autogenic training	Neuroleptics ('major' tranquillisers)
Transcendental meditation	Benzodiazepines ('minor' tranquillisers)
Progressive muscle relaxation	Nicotine
Biofeedback	Cannabis
Aromatherapy	Alcohol
Massage	Binge eating
Flotation tanks	Anodyne TV (soaps etc.)
Herbal baths	Escapism
Yoga	Hopi ear candling

The stress industry tells you that if you're not relaxed, you are in mortal danger. You not only have 'stress' but you could succumb to the scores of conditions they claim are 'stress-related' (just about any health irregularity you care to name). And then the industry stands by with its potted endocrinology, its thermometers, its squeezy balls, its 'stress dots', counselling and calming courses to fail to cure you.

Emotional arousal of any kind is currently called 'stress'. Even being excited about a promotion or a holiday is said to be 'stressful'. This is not only misleading and ridiculous, but malign. Because there are hundreds of different and opposite things that go by the name of 'stress', when we keep using the s-word we are constantly giving ourselves the message that *not* being calm is abnormal and pathological.

We need to revert to the kind of descriptive words all previous generations used to describe their feelings, before the theory of 'stress management' came along.

Normal words to describe our emotions

worry	exasperation
frustration	exhaustion
fear	tiredness
confusion	getting upset
guilt	anger
annoyance	desperation
irritation	despair
embarrassment	shock
tension	feeling overstretched
apprehension	hurrying
nervousness	being very busy
feeling 'hot under the collar'	etc.

These are not only more accurate but non-medical.

Official 'calm-down' warnings

There is a direct connection between 'stress management' and the current depression epidemic. Calm-down drugs, for example, work by chemically suppressing and slowing down the activity of the brain. When I asked the Department of Health: 'Are tranquillisers depressant?' spokesman Steve Ryan replied:

*Tranquillisers are not a class of drug recognised by the DOH as such because there are different types, such as hypnotics, anxiolytics and barbiturates, **but in so far as drugs are intended to calm people down, then ultimately the answer is yes – they are depressant.**[2]*

The American Medical Association warns of the dangers:

Depressants include barbiturates (such as Amytal, Nembutal and Seconal), benzodiazepines (such as Valium, Librium and Rohypnol), and methaqualone (Quaalude). **Depressant drugs, commonly known as tranquillizers or sleeping pills, are prescribed by doctors to relieve anxiety and sleeplessness.** *In controlled doses these drugs produce a feeling of relaxation and well being. Large doses result in intoxication similar to drunkenness.*[3]

The stress management industry is not reactive, like the NHS or Florence Nightingale. It is *proactive*. It promotes 'stress awareness'. It tells people they are suffering from stress and that they must look out for signs and symptoms. It takes problems and feelings and medicalises them in order to profit. And it claims to have mountains of scientific evidence.

SLOPPY SCIENCE

Today we look for our wisdom on human emotions and their consequences not to William Shakespeare, who laid bare the human soul, but to a man who tortured 1,400 rats a week in his Montreal laboratory. His name was Hans Selye and he was Austro-Canadian and didn't speak terribly good English. In the 1930s he borrowed the term 'stress' from engineering, muddling up two different engineering concepts: 'stress' (force exerted on an object) and 'strain' (deformation caused by that force). Fellow scientists attacked his methodologies, yet Selye's 'stress' idea took off. Its vagueness suited researchers who were not worried about rigour and just wanted to get funding for their work on human health and emotions. Even the very latest branch of 'stress' research, PNI or psychoneuroimmunology, shows no significant improvement in its grasp of the very thing under investigation.

> **Flaws in the stress 'science'**
>
> *When I was a University of East Anglia research fellow working with scientists at their Centre for Environmental Risk, we looked at hundreds of studies and found many serious and invalidating flaws. These included major definition failure (having no fixed control term), adaptation of the control term to suit funding, poor logic (for example, 'It happened after it therefore it was caused by it'), confusion of arousal and resignation (a very dangerous flaw, since they are different biological mechanisms that impact very differently on the body), confusion of stimulus and response (opposites), reliance on animal models, reliance on self-report data, poor methodologies, lack of follow-up studies, inadequate control groups, small samples, false extrapolation, conclusions drawn on the basis of surmise and a mass of technical errors.*

If my research had simply shown that 'stress management' was bogus, I wouldn't have bothered to write the book. I knew the reception it would get, and that I would be accused of attacking 'stress sufferers' rather than exposing the powerful multi-million pound industry that is deceiving them about their normal emotions and mechanisms.

When people are constantly being told alarmist nonsense that they are going to die, and that they must avoid 'stress' when they don't know exactly what it is, they become hyper-vigilant (over-alert) about their health. When they say they are 'stressed' or 'stressed out' they are really experiencing fear and anxiety:

- that they can't cope with life's demands

- that they are about to break down mentally or physically

- that they need to avoid arousal

- that they need to calm down.

These fears and anxieties have not happened by accident. They have been deliberately engendered by the stress management industry itself spreading myths about our health and our feelings.

Popular stress myths

'Stress is bad, pressure is good'

How come? Because stress is pressure you don't like, and pressure is stress you do?

'Stress causes disease'

That very much depends on what you mean by 'stress'. If you mean fight-or-flight, the stress research itself doesn't show that arousal causes disease. It shows that helplessness and apathy cause disease. If you mean being in a hurry or being very busy, research on anti-ageing suggests that time pressure and challenges increase the production of heatshock proteins that repair damaged cells and prolong life, a process known as hormesis. As we age this process slows down, but experts like Dr Marios Kyriazis say that seeking out challenges and rushing about 'exercise' the vital repair mechanism.[4]

'We work harder now'

We are apparently 'worse off than previous generations'. Under the 1834 Poor Law there were 600 workhouses in Britain. Compared with present-day worries, such as not having time to read the 11-section Daily Telegraph, *they had it tough. Up north people got up at three in the morning and clattered to work at mills in their clogs. People were 'clemmed' (frozen and starved) to death. Down south Daniel Defoe was in a debtors' prison and Charles Dickens was working in a boot-blacking factory at the age of 12. Children were up chimneys and down mines. People laboured in William Blake's 'dark Satanic mills' for barely enough to buy bread and potatoes.*

'The pace of life is faster now'

Our brains can't cope, say the stress merchants. Well, past generations also had peculiar conditions supposedly caused by the pace of life: 'brain fag', neurasthenia, nervous debility, 'nerves'. A typical sufferer was Mrs Bennet in Jane Austen's Pride and Prejudice, *written in 1813: 'I am frightened out of my wits; and have such tremblings, such flutterings, all over me, such spasms in my side, and pains in my head, and such beatings at heart, that I can get no rest by night or day.'*

We are not really more nervous or frenetic or hard-working now than past generations. These are all myths.

On the other hand, stress management can kill.

Kava kava, a herbal stress remedy, has been linked to fatalities from liver damage. Benzodiazepines, so-called 'minor' tranquillisers, extrapolating from Home Office statistics between 1964 and 2004, were involved in 17,000 deaths. How come? The American Medical Association explains:

> All depressants have a high potential for abuse. Tolerance to depressants develops quickly and may lead to physical and/or psychological dependence. These drugs work by temporarily shutting down some areas of the central nervous system; the user who takes increasingly large doses as tolerance develops risks the central nervous system shutting down entirely. This risk becomes particularly acute when depressants are combined with alcohol, which produces a synergistic effect – a phenomenon best understood as 'one plus one equals three.' Because the lethal dose of depressants remains the same as tolerance increases, a person taking heavy doses of depressants or mixing them with alcohol risks coma or death.[5]

One very popular 'stress' remedy available *without* prescription is alcohol – yet another chemical depressant that dulls the mind and can lead to depression, mental illness and death. Nicotine absorbed quickly or in high doses, is a depressant. One could go on ...

All this is very insulting to the human brain. As we shall see, it revels in engaging with the world and rewards us for having the courage to face up to our problems. Accepting life's challenges and completing tasks provides not just *real* relaxation (as distinct from the artificial kind) but what is infinitely more satisfying – *resolution* – as well.

NOTES

1. Professor Lightman speaking on *Equinox: The Science of Stress*, Channel 4, November 2000.

2. Department of Health, Information Line, 7 April 2004.

3. American Medical Association, Medical Library, 1999.

4. See Marios Kyriazis, *The Anti-Aging Plan*. Element Books, 2000.

5. American Medical Association Library statement 1999.

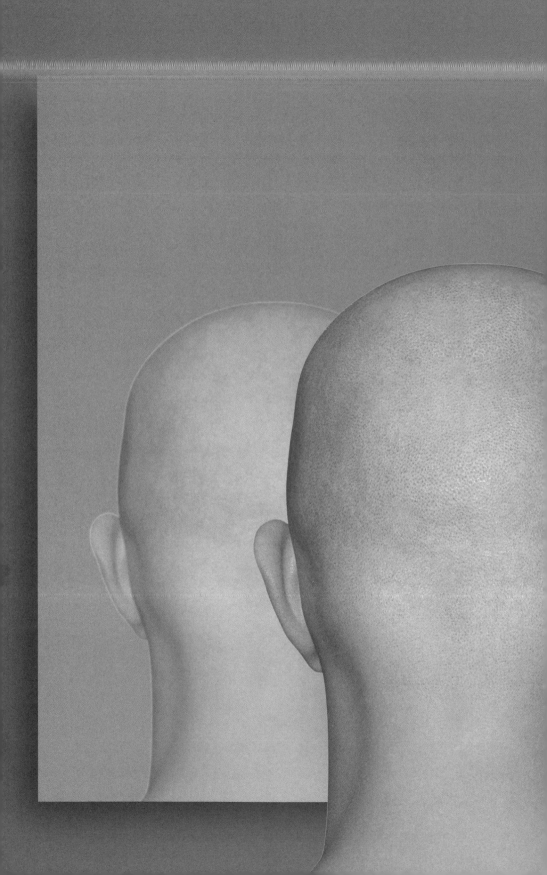

Crises and revelations

Many people who are suffering from despair have turned their backs on an impending crisis that they are unable or unwilling to face.

ESCAPIST STRATEGIES

Personal crises can be terrifying and make us feel physically ill. They seem to threaten our very identity, and this is why we often choose to avoid the serious problems that give rise to them. Escapists know in their hearts that the crisis is coming, that it is out there waiting to be faced and resolved, but they distract themselves in the hope that it may go away. It doesn't go away. Instead what happens to escapists is this:

1 They gradually sink into a trough of numbness and denial.

2 Even their desires and needs become muffled and vague.

3 They grow apathetic, craven and dishonest in their habits, both with other people and themselves.

4 They lose confidence and self-esteem.

5 Hope looks like a candle blinking out in the distance until finally ...

6 They feel desolate and see no way forward.

Running away from serious problems sends feedback to the brain that we are flustered and defenceless. This naturally increases our fear, so we have to run farther and faster. Eventually reality must be faced. But the result may surprise you. Every crisis offers an opportunity, a learning curve, from which we may emerge stronger and wiser and happier than we have ever been.

Personal crisis: W. G. Wilson

William Griffith Wilson, an ex-soldier and successful Wall Street businessman, drank to alleviate depression. By 1933 he had become an unemployable alcoholic, living on charity in Brooklyn. Incarcerated for the fourth time at Manhattan's Towns Hospital the following year, Wilson lay awake in his bed, terrified. He had reached a crisis of inner torment worse than anything even he had felt before in which he was struggling with his ideas and feelings. He expected the worst. But then suddenly he saw a flash of white light and felt a profound religious certainty. The epiphany changed his life. He never drank again. Wilson went on to found Alcoholics Anonymous and the revolutionary 'twelve-step programme' that has helped millions of alcoholics to kick the habit.

Personal crisis: Timothy Gallwey

Tennis player Tim Gallwey crashed his car into a snow-bank driving towards northern Maine. It was around midnight and 20 degrees below zero, and he had only the sports jacket he was wearing. He had no map or mobile phone and the last town had disappeared behind him 20 minutes ago. He got out and started walking but the cold hurt his ears. He tried to run but the cold sapped his strength. He realised that he was probably about to die:

I found myself saying aloud, 'Okay, if now is the time, so be it. I'm ready.' I really meant it. With that I stopped thinking about it and began walking calmly down the road, suddenly aware of the beauty of the night. I became absorbed in the silence of the stars and in the loveliness of the dimly lit forms around me; everything was beautiful. Then without thinking, I started running. To my surprise I didn't stop for a full forty minutes, and then only because I spotted a light burning in the window of a distant house.[1]

Gallwey didn't die frozen in the snow. He invented a Zen meditative technique for playing tennis without thinking called the 'Inner Game'. It made him rich and famous.

REVELATIONS AND EPIPHANIES

These two stories illustrate an experience that has happened to a great many of us: a sudden moment of calm, clarity and visionary joy that occurs at the very climax of a personal crisis or when people seem to be facing imminent death (when the revelations are called NDEs or 'Near Death Experiences'). As we know, these epiphanies are actively *sought out* by religious devotees who put themselves through fasting, scourging and climbing up into high mountains to try to achieve them. But they can occur naturally to those who are not at all religious, and to people of all ages and cultural backgrounds.

Author's epiphany

I had such an experience myself when I was young. I was starting out as a writer, living with my parents, and I was suffering from panic attacks that were becoming more and more distressing. I could not take drugs because my father was addicted to sedatives and I saw what they had done to him. My habit had been to try to escape the symptoms by surrounding myself with friends and keeping busy. But nights were terrifying spirals and I feared for my sanity. One evening I decided I couldn't outrun this any more: I was too exhausted. I would turn and face the monster. So I went to my room, lay down and waited for the worst. I remember that I actually folded my arms. Suddenly, instead of terror, I felt absolute peace. I went downstairs and looked at my violent, drug-addicted father watching a film on television: On the Waterfront. *I was overwhelmed with a feeling of love and pity for my father, admiration for the film, gratitude for our tiny council house, the lamp on the television, the world I lived in. Everything suddenly made sense. I never suffered from panic attacks again.*

'COMPLEXITY SCIENCE'

How can the brain, at the very height of a crisis that threatens to disintegrate us, suddenly convulse its powers like this and produce a life-changing revelation? Neurologists haven't really fathomed this out yet, but one group of exceptionally gifted scientists at the Santa Fe Institute in New Mexico have produced exhilarating research that gives us a clue.

Nobel Prize-winners like Murray Gell-Mann, Philip Anderson and Kenneth Arrow have been studying what are technically known as 'complex systems'.

Examples of complex systems are:

piles of sand

pans of simmering water

the money markets

artificial intelligence

insect swarms

bird flocks

tornados

storm clouds

etc.

All of these systems exhibit a strange transition that the scientists have named *emergence*.

At the highest point of tension and on the very edge of chaos, they 'change gear' and spontaneously produce *order*.

Example of emergence

A pan of water is put on to boil. All the little water molecules behave more and more randomly and chaotically until suddenly, as though at the throwing of a switch, they all organise themselves into a hexagonal convection pattern and simmer. From the very edge of chaos emerges order.

Nothing to do with me, you might think. Except that one of the complex systems under study is the human brain.

Undergoing tension and resolution may be absolutely crucial to its vital work of making connections. The nervousness that our stress-managed age has come to fear and avoid may actually be part of a complex process designed to produce a heightened version of our abilities. This would certainly explain why creative people go through an emotional loop to produce their best work and why they so often need what they call pressure, or a deadline, in order to bring forth their magic.

Rossini's crescendos

Gioacchino Rossini (famous for the crescendos in his music such as the William Tell Overture) *couldn't compose until the night before the performance. Once he composed on the actual day of the performance, with the impresario's henchmen standing over him as he wrote and threatening to throw him out of an upstairs window. What was happening to poor Rossini during these scary creative episodes?*

THE BRAIN'S BATTLE STATIONS

When we face a threat or challenge, the body goes into the complex 'fight-or-flight response', triggered by the hypothalamus at the back of the brain as it galvanises us into action. Stress management people are fond of telling us that this is a 'very primitive' threat mechanism, suitable for fighting sabre-tooth tigers but inappropriate for our modern lives. The mechanism is *in fact* highly sophisticated. This is just some of what happens.

Yellow alert

The hypothalamus transmits electrical and chemical signals to the pituitary gland. The pituitary relays the exciting news to the adrenal glands just above the kidneys using the hormone ACTH (Adreno-Cortico-Trophic Hormone). Over 30 chemical messengers suddenly cascade from the adrenal glands and are sent round the body. Their tiny tasks are complex: they can alter metabolism, alter blood pressure, alter the pigmentation of the skin and raise blood sugar levels. The main effects are:

- *the heart rate increases*
- *metabolism of sugars increases*
- *blood thickens*
- *blood pressure rises*
- *hands and feet lose heat*
- *sweating increases*
- *the mouth becomes dry*
- *muscles tense*
- *digestion is disrupted giving rise to ...*
- *'butterflies', diarrhoea and nausea.*

Red alert

Blood supply is being diverted away from the extremities and non-essential systems like digestion. Why? The blood is needed elsewhere. Of course some of it must go to the large muscles, which may be needed for fighting or fleeing. But this emergency blood boost must also flow elsewhere. It must go to the brain, which literally experiences a 'rush of blood', although this is carefully controlled by the surrounding vascular system or you might have an aneurism. The body may be preparing for action, but the brain is readying itself to work in a high gear, to focus, connect, create, crystallise and come up with appropriate solutions to this emergency.

Lift-off

Within the brain's own circuitry an electrical charge now goes down the tiny main cable or 'axon' of each affected nerve cell and crosses the synaptic gap to neighbouring cells and circuits – sometimes on a very grand scale. The bigger the connection, the bigger the brainwave and the bigger the epiphany we may experience. The brain is signalling to us that it is making sense of our reality. There is even a metaphorical language that we use to describe our feelings during crises, of which 'pressure', 'rush of blood', 'seeing red' and 'don't burst a blood vessel' are among hundreds of examples.[2]

This miraculous process is evidently the source of our brainwaves, our peak experiences, our epiphanies. The brain changes gear when we face threats and challenges. It has to. It is designed to help us survive and learn. This is why it is wired to produce brilliant ideas when we are in the middle of bad experiences. This is also why most of our leisure pursuits, as we shall see later on, are designed to bring us to *artificial* crises and climaxes, and give us what we call an adrenalin rush or a 'buzz'.

THE LIGHT AT THE END OF THE TUNNEL

Without the complex physiological changes that go by the name of 'nervousness', the brain would not be able to move into its higher gears, or orchestrate its key connections, or create its brainwaves, or manage its crisis thinking. People would just go bumbling along from day to day without ever having access to its special powers. This is why creative professionals like writers and composers tend to live on the edge or 'on their nerves'. This is where they find their brains function at their optimum capacity and where they can produce their magic.

You can use this knowledge when you yourself face a crisis. It may help you get through and appreciate the true powers of your brain and its workings. As Othello puts it in Shakespeare's play of the same name:

> ... O my soul's joy!
> If after every tempest come such calms,
> May the winds blow till they have waken'd death!
> And let the labouring bark climb hills of seas
> Olympus-high, and duck again as low
> As hell's from heaven! If it were now to die,
> 'Twere now to be most happy, for I fear
> My soul hath her content so absolute
> That not another moment like to this
> Succeeds in unknown fate.
>
> (William Shakespeare, *Othello*, Act II)

NOTES

1. W. Timothy Gallwey, *The Inner Game of Tennis*. Jonathan Cape, 1975, p. 138.

2. Angela Patmore, *The Truth About Stress*, Grove Atlantic, 2006, pp. 348–50.

Stop 'giving up the ghost'

8

My reputation as a Heartless Bitch will perhaps have forewarned you that this is one book on depression where you won't get an easy ride. Unlike many of my fellow advisers on mental health issues, I'm not trying to calm you down or mollycoddle your feelings. I regard it as my responsibility to get you to face the Demon of Despair, deal with it robustly and truly get better. I happen to think you are more likely to do this if you face reality than if you face somewhere else, pop pills and imagine calm scenes.

So this chapter has to start by giving you a fright.

> **Health warning**
> *Hopeless and helpless people should understand that, even if they have never attempted suicide, they may be allowing themselves to get sick and even to die by their failure to help themselves.*

Research on despair shows that it makes the sufferer vulnerable to harmful physiological changes. In America in the 1970s, depressed patients were interviewed about their feelings while they were wired up to monitoring equipment, and the scientists found that even *talking* about feelings of hopelessness and helplessness may cause a sudden drop in blood pressure sufficient to be life-threatening, even though the speaker may be completely unaware of any physiological change.[1]

Earlier, in the late 1960s, Martin Seligman and Steven Maier carried out experiments that were to change the face of modern psychology. Seligman and Maier discovered that:

1 If they exposed laboratory animals or human volunteers to painful situations, their normal response was to try to escape and avoid the pain. This was not unexpected.

2 If they could not escape, most of them gradually resigned themselves and exhibited apathetic behaviour. This was not unexpected either.

3 What was unexpected was that even if an escape hatch was then provided, some of these pathetic subjects continued to behave in a resigned way, putting up with the pain and not trying to save themselves.

Afterwards their resignation was found to have quite dramatically undermined their health. It became clear that giving up is maladaptive and harmful to survival because it disrupts the body's defences and exposes it to pathogens. The scientists called the behaviour they had seen 'learned helplessness' or 'failure to initiate responses in the face of threat'.[2] Martin Seligman went on to develop a model of depression based on his experimental work.

RESIGNATION, NOT 'STRESS'
Resignation is quite different from arousal. In fact the reaction is the biological *opposite* of the fight-or-flight response designed to galvanise our brains and bodies to meet challenges (that many are now calling 'stress'). Learned helplessness, in contrast, is a kind of biological death wish. It is very useful, for example, to a gazelle about to face imminent slaughter by a predator. Resignation numbs the threatened creature by releasing opiate-like substances in the brain to calm it for its impending ugly fate. It acts as an anaesthetic and as a painkiller. The fact that the response shuts off the immune system (called 'auto-immune suppression') is perhaps no surprise: if you are just about to die, you hardly need an immune system.

THE STING IN THE TAIL
The sting in the tail is this: if an animal – or indeed a person – is *not* facing imminent violent destruction, the helpless response shuts off the immune system *anyway*. It kills while it calms. Meanwhile all attempts at self-help appear futile, because opiate-like natural substances known as pentapeptides are being released into the nervous system to anaesthetise the inert individual from present pain and

future action. This is why, in humans, helplessness is likely to increase feelings of pointlessness, desolation and despair.

There is robust research evidence on the health consequences of resignation from studies of prisoners of war, survivors of concentration camps (describing those who had succumbed) and bereaved spouses. Insurance companies are familiar with the potentially lethal effects on middle-aged men who 'give up the ghost' having lost their jobs. Their survival can no longer be guaranteed.

Helplessness – a case study

In my work as a Restart trainer, I often came across jobseekers who had 'given up', not only on looking for work but on everything else as well. So I would read them a press clipping to illustrate the potentially lethal consequences of resignation. The article was about 27-year-old Andrew Thomas of Glamorgan, who died after being made redundant. Pathologist Dr David Stock said Mr Thomas appeared to have been 'a completely healthy young man' and the cause of his death was 'unascertainable'. After initial attempts to find work, Mr Thomas had begun getting up late and spending every day watching videos and television. He even gave up getting dressed and would sit all day in his pyjamas. His father Gwilym was reported to have said after the hearing, 'I believe he lost the will to live.'[3]

The learned helplessness research may clarify the mystery of what 'stress' scientists mistakenly and inaccurately refer to as 'long-term stress', which they blame for harming our health. The confusion has led to a great deal of misinformation being given to the public about 'stress' arousal and disease links. People are being constantly warned about the fight-or-flight response – a survival mechanism that can save them – and *not* warned about the opposite response – resignation – that can kill them.

THE HELPLESS PROFILE

How does somebody suffering from despair identify this helpless mindset? Here are some of the attributes typical of the helpless personality:

- low self-esteem

- poor coping skills

- 'can't be bothered' attitude

- avoidance of 'scenes' or conflict

- unwillingness to face problems head on

- submission (often with resentment)

- escapist calming habits, e.g. alcohol, nicotine, etc.

- escapist games-playing, television, DVD-watching, etc.

- not fighting back

- resigned and apathetic attitude

- fatalism ('what will be will be').

Helpless individuals will resort to strategies that avoid confronting problems or threats, preferring to cling to calming 'painkilling' habits like tobacco, cannabis, alcohol and comfort-eating, even though they know these to be potentially harmful to their health. The resigned person simply doesn't care. He or she hears all the time comments from others that they are 'hopeless' – and indeed they are. Their fate generally hangs in the balance, or by a seriously disabled spider's last cobweb. A common phrase used in my classes was *I can't be arsed*. The helpless have given up trying to save themselves and turned their back on a threatening situation. This approach to life is not only abject but extremely dangerous.

HELPLESS THINKING

Do the following thoughts occur to you? Tick the relevant boxes and score yourself on each statement.

	Always	Often	Sometimes	Never
	5	3	1	0

	Always	Often	Sometimes	Never
1. I can't summon the energy lately.				
2. I doubt if this will help me. Nothing ever does.				
3. I've always been unlucky.				
4. It might have worked when I was young.				
5. If I had my way I'd just stay in bed.				
6. I don't have ambitions, just jobs.				
7. I had a bad start, and never looked forward.				
8. Secretly I believe I'm finished.				
9. I feel happiest when I'm asleep.				
10. I just cannot be bothered.				
11. I doze in the daytime as I'm always tired.				
12. Avoiding problems is better than worrying about them.				
13. I don't cook just for myself.				
14. However normal I seem, inwardly I feel utterly defeated.				
15. I don't open worrying letters (I put them behind the clock etc.).				
16. I drink to drown my sorrows.				
17. I start things but then lose interest.				
18. If anybody asks my advice, I just shrug.				
19. People say I'm negative, but why fake being jolly?				
20. I have problems but I try not to think about them.				
21. I've given up asking for help as you don't get it.				
22. Taking risks scares me so I've stopped taking them.				
23. Like the song says, I'm 'tired of living but scared of dying'.				

	Always	Often	Sometimes	Never
24. If you don't try, you don't get disappointed.				
25. At least I don't show myself up by trying and failing.				
26. Once bitten, twice shy. That's why I'm shy.				
27. It doesn't matter what you look like when you get to my age.				
28. I sigh a lot.				
29. My home is a tip and that used to bother me.				
30. If I didn't smoke I couldn't cope.				

Scores

0–45   Even though you may be depressed right now you are really self-determining. You are a survivor and make your own luck.

45–80   You don't give up easily. When disaster strikes you will generally find out how to cope.

80–115   You are prone to letting others decide your fate. Stand your ground and make the effort. *You* decide.

115–150   You have the most to gain by changing, as your whole life is waiting out there for you. Stop drifting over the waterfall. Wake up and take control *right now*.

HOW *NOT* TO BE HELPLESS

So what can you do if your habits are helpless as well as hopeless? Use this panel: photocopy it or cut it out and paste it on the wall. Send it to yourself as an e-mail. Stick it on your mirror. Nail it to the back gate. It is very important.

The first step is REALISATION.

Understand and recognise what your behaviour is doing to you, and to your body, and that you are committing slow-motion suicide.

The second step is to TAKE CONTROL.

So long as you act helpless and 'give up', you relinquish control of your life to others, and to chance. Take back control. Be the master of your fate. This is your life. Live it.

The third step is to STOP TRYING TO ESCAPE.

Don't try to outrun reality – you'll never make it! In the long run, and even the short run, escapist behaviour won't make you safer. It won't even make you feel more secure, because it lowers your self-esteem and leaves you vulnerable. You render yourself defenceless in a scary place. And meanwhile, the problem itself gets bigger with time because you have failed to address it.

The last step is to learn the simple truth: BEST TO FACE THE WORST.

Turn and embrace challenges. Face problems head on. Our whole culture is full of examples of facing down monsters and robbing them of their power because as a race we have learned this generally works. When we run from monsters, they grow. When we turn and face them, they diminish. Whatever the problem or threat you are trying to avoid, it is unlikely to be as dangerous to your mind and body as the harm you are doing to yourself. The moment you make the decision to get off your behind and help yourself, you will feel a surge of energy. Try it – you'll like it. You will feel different because your brain will support you. Remember: it is designed to help you survive.

THE NEED FOR PRESSURE

If resignation is nature's way of anaesthetising us, what does this tell us about the opposite, more proactive style of living such as:

- facing reality

- accepting challenges

- meeting threats

- taking action

- defending ourselves?

All of these behaviours are natural because they are all survival-motivated. In the wild, whether you are a mountain gorilla or a meerkat, you will struggle every day to survive, to find food and water, to defend yourself, your kin and your territory, to find a mate and reproduce. A lot of your life will therefore naturally be *arousing, scary, painful and worrying,* and a lot of your energy will be spent *rushing about, licking your wounds, disputing, displaying and socialising.*

So it is with people. A lot of what we do to survive must necessarily involve a certain amount of 'pressure' – emotional activity, nervousness, being in a hurry, responding quickly to the demands of life, doing things that make us apprehensive, angry or afraid. According to the theory of 'managing stress' these activities and feelings *are all bad for us.* Because they trigger arousal, they must be unhealthy. And because they are unhealthy they must be avoided.

So now you see why 'stress management' may have got you into your present avoidant and inactive state. Pressure has something to do with feeling depressed, certainly. But it is not the pressure itself, so much as the *avoidance* that may have brought you low.

Remember: Depression may mean insufficient pressure
rather than too much!

BULLYING

It can hardly surprise anyone, in an age of emotion alleviation and arousal management, that bullying is on the increase. According to an HSE technical report on workplace bullying, for example, 40% of victims do not even turn to anyone for support. They simply bow their necks or leave.[4] This craven behaviour actually *encourages* bullying in the workplace. The proliferation of anti-bullying websites and charities – although it may help 'victims' to understand the injustice they have suffered – fails to address the underlying cause. Bullies generally pick on those who look like victims: people who are passive and meek, who do not complain and do not fight back. In other words, they choose people who are helpless in the first place. Don't be helpless.

- Stand up straight and tall – don't look as though you are about to roll into a ball out of sheer fright. Hold your head up.

- Courteously assert yourself. Listen to them, register that you have listened, but say that you have the right to be treated with respect, just as they do. Ask them questions. Why are they behaving like this?

- Don't display emotion. Keep your fears to yourself.

- Meet the gaze of bullies. Don't look at your shoes.

- Whatever you are feeling inside, speak calmly and clearly.

- Repeat yourself in different words if they ignore you.

- Afterwards, make a note of what was said and retain documents, faxes and e-mails sent to you, with dates and, if there were any, witnesses.

- If you feel the situation is actually dangerous and you can't handle it yourself, consult those who can: management, the Citizens Advice Bureau (CAB), your union, school authorities.

- Don't just let things fester. If you do you may eventually 'snap' and lose your temper. Unless you like fights, use assertion, *not* aggression.

You will find more on assertiveness in the Challenge programme.

NOTES

1. J. J. Lynch, *The Broken Heart: The Medical Consequences of Loneliness*. Basic Books, 1977; J. J. Lynch, K. E. Lynch and E. Friedmann, 'A cry unheard: sudden reductions in blood pressure while talking about feelings of hopelessness and helplessness', *Integrative Physiological and Behavioral Science*, 27 (2), 1992, pp. 151–69; J. J. Lynch, *The Language of the Heart: The Human Body in Dialogue*. Basic Books, 1985; J. J. Lynch, S. A. Thomas *et al.*, 'Blood pressure changes while talking', *Journal of Nervous and Mental Disease*, 168, 1980, pp. 526–34.

2. M. E. P. Seligman and S. F. Maier, 'Failure to escape traumatic shock', *Journal of Experimental Psychology*, 74, 1967, pp. 1–9; M. E. P. Seligman, *Helplessness: On Depression, Development and Death*. Freeman, 1975.

3. 'Tragedy of man with only TV to live for', *Daily Mail*, 19 April 1997.

4. HSE, *A 'Management Standards' Approach to Tackling Work-Related Stress*, Part I, p. 14.

Accepting loss

9

One of the main reasons why people slump into despair is loss. Loss knocks us sideways. Everything suddenly goes quiet. We feel as though we have been in an accident, and it takes time for the brain to work out what's going on. As the poet Emily Dickinson so timelessly put it: *At leisure is the soul that gets a staggering blow.*

If it is of any relevance, your Heartless Bitch has experienced loss herself. I have been homeless, I have been made redundant, I have been dumped and rejected in love, I have faced crippling debt and more than once I have been bereaved. So I am not going to get on your case or shout 'snap out of it'. What I will do is try to give you some fresh ideas on the subject. You don't have to sink into a peat bog so long as you take action to help yourself.

COMING TO TERMS WITH LOSS

What do friends mean when they say we eventually 'come to terms' with loss? Is it just a saying designed to reassure us and make us feel better? Do they have any idea what we are going through? After all, we have been insulted by fate. When we were children we were promised there would always be happy endings. Now we find this was a lie. Of course we don't suddenly 'reach a peaceful settlement' with loss, or say 'fair enough'. It isn't fair at all. What really happens is that day by day the realisation slowly dawns on us that, whether we like it or not, what is lost is not coming back. We may not like it, but so long as we try to deny and avoid this realisation, we cannot move on. We live a twilight existence. We are facing the past, using all our emotional strength to try to pull it into the present. Let the line go. Live in the present. Face the future. Though you may not realise it right now, you do have one.

Once we have the courage to accept the truth, the pain changes. It still hurts, but it modifies into a far less distressing emotion. The experience becomes something we can begin to understand and place in the context of our lives. Human beings are not designed for permanent grief. We are designed for survival. In the end we make an adjustment, and this is nature's way.

SELF-PITY

Self-pity is a destructive emotion. It prolongs the pain and demoralises the person who gives in to it because it lowers your spirits and makes you feel defeated, weary and fatigued. Consider what tears are for. Nature gave us lachrymal glands for crying, to communicate with others that we are sad. It's a defence mechanism because other people need to know not to be unkind to us just when we are feeling fragile.

Crying is quite natural when we have experienced loss. But tears also make your eyes tired. This is so that you feel inclined to 'sleep it off' and rest up for a while to recharge your batteries. Then when you wake up, it's time to start afresh and get on with life. On the other hand, if you misuse this natural response by continually sorrowing and weeping, you'll *keep* feeling as though you want to close the curtains and go back to bed. You won't have any energy or motivation at all.

Self-pity is also utterly undignified. 'Look at me, I'm really suffering. *Woe, woe and thrice woe.*' Yes, we know you're suffering. We've all suffered. It's not a competition in which you have to prove your pain is worse than anybody else's. Besides, if you keep reflecting back your own misery like a fairground mirror, crying, playing sad tunes and staring into the abyss, you are sapping your own strength to recover.

Once you decide to survive, your brain will turn on its magical powers again (it switches them off out of sheer boredom when you can't be bothered), and new ideas and connections will begin to blossom in your mind. Don't sit there in a pool of toxic tears. I'm not just being a Scary Mary: you need to be told these things or you'll wallow indefinitely.

TYPES OF LOSS

There are many kinds of loss. What I'd like you to do right now is 'rate' the following 20 kinds of loss, in order of emotional impact you think they make, according to your own experience and knowledge.

- Bereavement (immediate family)
- Contest (as in sport)
- Companion animal
- Employment
- Fight
- Hair
- Health
- Hearing
- Home
- Limbs
- Liberty
- Looks
- Love partner
- Material possessions
- Miscarriage
- Mobility
- Money
- Sight
- Teeth
- Youth

These are just 20 of the many possible losses I could have chosen. Some may mean nothing to you. Others may loom forth as *the* most devastating experience anyone could possibly have. But they have all, somewhere, sometime, broken somebody's heart. It depends on what you hold most dear.

When you have made your assessment, look at the top three. The likelihood is that they have happened to you, and this is why you understand their impact. One of them may well be the cause of your despair. But whatever your ratings of the losses on the list, it is important for you to understand that, in a sense, *they are one and the same.*

LOSS ITSELF

Loss may be deeply personal, but it is also generic. Losing is one thing all human beings know about. It is what we do as we go through life. As you get older, bits fall off. We lose our careers, our prospects, our health, our teeth, our hair, our eyesight, our hearing, our looks, our youth, our mobility, our loved ones and finally, for many of us, our possessions and our homes. We may also lose our dreams, which can hurt most of all. Coping with loss is therefore par for the course for children and grown-ups. We do it all the time.

You are literally surrounded by people who have lost what they treasured. My Restart trainees had lost jobs, livelihoods, homes, families, freedom and self-respect. I could certainly help them with the last one, though they had to deal with the others themselves, using their courage and intelligence.

No matter how it hurts, we can learn from enlightened people who willingly relinquish their precious possessions. Some of them simply 'give it all away' and enter a monastic order. Some join a community where everything belongs to everybody. Those who are devoutly religious believe that if you give up all the things you hold dear, the sacrifice doesn't leave you with nothing. By a mysterious logic it leaves you with *everything*, because you become a spiritual person. In fact devout people think that it is only when we *have* relinquished everything that we are currently grasping on to that we truly find ourselves. They may quote from the Bible (Ecclesiastes 5:15 and Job 1:21) and say:

As he came forth from his mother's womb, naked shall he return.

Or they may say:

You have to lose yourself in order to find yourself.

Even if you are not ready to go to such spiritual lengths, you can try these three initiatives:

1 When you have lost precious things in the past, how did you manage *then*? Write down what you did. If you keep a diary, look back and see how you coped. Be honest: don't belittle your former feelings and assume they hurt less than your feelings now. Get some perspective.

2 The loss that hurts you most may *also* have happened to someone you know reasonably well. If you haven't already done so, talk to them. Find out how *they* coped. What did they have to do to get through the experience, to survive? Go on the Internet and ask people there. You will find kindred spirits who have not only shared your experience, but who may be further on in the healing process than you are and can pierce the gloom.

3 To make you realise how restricting 'clinging on to possessions' can be, try *giving away something that you value*. The feeling may surprise you. In the wild, animals can act possessive, for example over a carcass or a mate, but mostly they travel light. Having lots of belongings would seriously impair their freedom.

Disabled heroes – 1
Christopher Reeve broke his neck in a riding accident. In his dreams he could still walk and run, though in reality he knew he was a quadriplegic. He never gave up hope of a cure, and became an inspiration to others by carrying on with his career and setting a high benchmark for other equally disabled people.

Disabled heroes – 2
The Paralympians compete on a world stage at the highest level and hone their skills, not to come second, but to win.

Disabled heroes – 3
Battle Back, an organisation that rehabilitates war-wounded soldiers, including double and triple amputees, offers them thrilling adventure activities that give them back their self-esteem and joie de vivre. *If you go on their website you can find out how some of them transformed themselves into the positive people they are now.*

MOURNING

Grief is not a disease. Nor is it a sign of mental illness. Grief is normal to all living creatures when they have suffered loss. You don't have to take a pill for grief. If you do, the natural process of grieving could be mutated or extended. When we grieve we are undergoing change, and we are growing new wings, because our old ones have been battered about. If you give it time, the whole sad process will slowly make sense to you.

Sometimes people go on mourning because they are ashamed to stop. They think this would tarnish the love they feel for the individual they have lost, or demonstrate that they were somehow insufficiently devoted. Don't be ashamed to move on. Even elephants, after they have stood round a fallen comrade sometimes for days, caressing the body gently with their trunks, eventually go on their way and continue with their lives. The seasons come and go, and the rhythm of life moves us forward. Be natural. Go with it.

My dear cousin Brian lost six members of his family – his wife Sandra, his mum Kath, his son Lee and three little grandchildren, in an arson attack on their home in Chingford, East London. When the site where their house used to stand was cleared, Brian found comfort in creating a small memorial garden there with trees and little plaques to his loved ones. He also raised money to buy two incubators for the maternity ward where the grandchildren were born. There was a small ceremony on the ward when the equipment was dedicated, and no one will ever forget it. Doing these kind and constructive things helped Brian to find the strength and the sanity to rebuild his life.

FIVE LITTLE LIFELINES

Here are five simple remedial actions to help you deal with loss. They are all methods that have proven successful for real people in real despair.

Keep a journal

Winston Churchill kept a journal and used it to get some perspective on his worst experiences. Try this yourself. Write down what you feel, day by day. Be honest. If you cry on the page, wipe it with a tissue and carry on writing. *We have to compose our thoughts in order to put them on paper, and this is a healing process.*

Things to Do Today

Every morning when you wake up, give yourself a list of 'Things to Do Today'. You may not do them all, but challenge yourself to accomplish at least one. It's like winding up a clock: you will feel the little wheels and cogs begin to grind into action.

Create a memorial

It doesn't have to be grand or expensive, but you can use your imagination to make something that pays a lasting tribute. An album of photographs with inscriptions, a book of memories you could post on the Internet, a painting, a plaque, a bench with an inscription, a feature tree in a special spot – these are just some of the ideas people have thought of to commemorate their loved ones.

Raise your morale

Your morale is important to your survival right now, so don't leave it to chance, or passing moods. In a war it is vital to keep people's spirits high or they will give up and lose. Take command, and take action that will make you feel positive. Choose something that has worked for you before, and put some *will* into it.

Tackle that task

One very good way to lift your spirits off the ground during loss is counter-intuitive, but it really worked for some of my trainees. It is this. *Go and find something that you have long put off, that you don't want to do, and do it.* You'll be surprised at the effect on your spirits: it's like hitting the bottom and bouncing back up. This is especially true if the task makes you nervous.

FOUR-LEGGED LOSS

Finally, if the person you have lost had four legs, of course you can't possibly *replace* him or her by getting another one. But there are thousands of unwanted animals in shelters around the country. Each one is an individual in its own right, with lots of love and faith to give. It's not their fault your beloved companion has gone, and they need a home, hope and kindness. They too are grieving for those they have lost. You might find a real friend in need there.

Going for the 'CC'

Depressed people tend to use games and leisure pursuits as displacement activities to avoid facing problems and challenges. If you use them for this and don't respect reality, or make the necessary changes in your lifestyle to deal with the real issues affecting your moods, you will stick where you are and not move forward. So this chapter is not about escaping, but about *exploring*.

> *Leisure pursuits can be very useful if you are in despair – provided you know how and why they work. But you need to understand the pay-off, and what games are actually designed to do before they can really enrich your mind.*

As we have seen in Chapter 7 on crises, the brain is very adept at orchestrating its connections and coming up with brainwaves and epiphanies at big moments and crossroads in our lives. Religious people have actively gone in search of these revelations by exposing themselves to unusual hardships – from wearing hair-shirts to walking across hot coals, and from self-flagellation and fasting to wandering alone in deserts. We know exciting revelations don't have to be left to chance (or to magic mushrooms either, in case that unworthy thought entered your noddle).

In our leisure pursuits, *artificial* versions of sublime religious revelations happen, and they happen quite deliberately. In fact we put ourselves in some version of harm's way in order to reach something *like* the soul-sensing experiences of religious faith, of Near Death Experiences, of Zen *sartori* or enlightenment. So for those of you who are hopelessly low right now, getting off your bottom and taking action to make you feel good may be easier and far more pleasurable than you think. You too can have 'wow' experiences.

THE AROUSAL CURVE

In all of our key leisure activities, in our literary classics, in drama, cinema, sport, music, adventure activities and rites of passage, the same exhilarating sequence emerges:

1 a steady build-up of tension

2 a peak of excitement or crescendo

3 a moment of clarity and realisation

4 resolution.

I call these extreme experiences CCs or 'cerebral climaxes'. My research, which spans 25 years in literature, sports psychology and the science on 'stress', highlights the importance to mental health and well-being of the CC. The theory of 'managing' our emotions by avoidance and calming down is really emotional censorship. It rubbishes our leisure pursuits, because despite our modern obsession with 'managing stress', people spend their spare time on climactic activities virtually guaranteed to involve tension, tears and fears.

They deliberately allow themselves to go on an emotional rollercoaster that climaxes in a crescendo, a result, a pay-off. The conventional wisdom is that we are all simply motivated by the pursuit of pleasure, but climactic activities are much more complex than that. They facilitate a so-called 'adrenalin rush', an arousal curve. They are purposely designed to give us 'highs'.

GOING FOR THE GOLDEN FEELING

People have always been willing to endure tension, tears and fears, so long as there is a climactic experience at the end of it. Falling in love can be highly distressing but few would forego the amazing cerebral climaxes that a love affair can give. Or consider the 1970s personal development programme known as EST (Erhard Seminar Training), the brainchild of Werner Erhard. Adopting the often abusive and demeaning approach of Zen master training, EST stripped away every layer of belief from trainees until they discovered within themselves a liberating, ego-less state known as 'It'.

The modern equivalent would be tense quizzes like *The Weakest Link*, in which Anne Robinson seeks to humiliate general knowledge buffs on national television. There is no shortage of contestants. Afterwards a lot of them say it gave them a buzz, and that they would 'highly recommend' the experience to anyone (over the age of 18. You can download entry forms by e-mailing weakestlink@bbc.co.uk – I gave them out to my trainees.

The need for the CC is very prevalent in human society. It may explain (explain, not forgive) certain self-destructive and anti-social acts such as gambling all the housekeeping or flirting with the forbidden. For most of us CCs are obtained more easily by taking part in leisure activities. The more extreme the activity, the higher the curve, but the pattern is always the same.

The brain's powers are heightened during CCs, and scientists now have a good idea why it navigates us towards them, rewarding us with goosebumps and spine-tinglings when we are willing to undergo a particularly big 'tension loop'. *Involuntary* loops that may occur during personal crises can provide the necessary tension–resolution pattern for an epiphany, a brainwave. If not, there is this lot listed below.

CC PURSUITS
Juveniles

- Childhood dares
- Fiction and fairy stories
- Gruesome spewsome comics
- Extreme computer games
- Teenage daredevil pursuits
- Romance and sex
- Fighting and disputing
- 'Recreational' drugs
- Fagging, 'hazing'
- Rites of passage

Adults

- Classics of fiction
- Thrillers & chillers
- Drama & theatre
- The horror movie
- Poetry
- Quizzes & contests
- Punchline jokes
- Hunting
- Spectator sports
- Participant sports
- Extreme sports
- Racing
- Martial arts
- Fitness workouts
- White-knuckle rides
- Adventure activities
- 'Drumroll' circus acts
- Gambling
- Classical music
- Challenges (mental & physical)
- Romance and sex

Ah, you may think: *romance and sex* – that explains it all. But cerebral climaxes are not some minor version of, or substitute for, sexual climaxes. They are better than sex. Religious devotees have foresworn sexuality to experience them, and adventurers put their very lives at risk. In fact, sex is a version of what cerebral climaxes are, because the body serves the brain, and in all its subsystems recognises its master. 'Frisson' is that exhilarating tension without which sex can be staid, and humans have turned sex into an art form just so that they can have lots of CCs. Animals just use it for making little animals.

ASSIGNMENT
Experience the CC yourself. Try the following:

A sports event, either as a spectator or – even better – a participant
Notice the build-up of tension that makes you nervous. Why is this worse if there is a nip-and-tuck contest? Why is a mismatch not exciting? If you like football, what do you feel when there is a draw, followed by a 'sudden death' result? Have you been cheated of genuine resolution?

A thriller

Choose a thriller, a real page-turner that is difficult to put down (you can find plenty of ads on the Amazon website or ask in your local library). Try to read it as quickly as possible rather than over several weeks. Notice the effect on your heart rate. Some thrillers, like Thomas Harris's novels *Silence of the Lambs* and *Red Dragon*, are advertised as heart-thumpers. How would you feel if somebody had torn out the last ten pages?

A movie

Choose a 'high-end' (clever and emotional) classic film rather than a cheap tricks, gore-and-guts, special-effects flick. Pick an epic like *Gladiator* or a classic sci-fi thriller like *Alien*, or a Hitchcock tension-building horror, or even a classic romance like *Gone with the Wind* or *Brief Encounter*. Big movies often feature a lead character who is put through very hell yet comes out of it genuinely heroic. But their main purpose is to arouse tension, climb to a climax and then resolve. Experience it and you'll see. My trainees were asked to draw a graph as the film went along – it can look like the temperature chart of a very sick patient!

A musical classic

Listen to one of the following:

- Bach: Toccata and Fugue in D Minor
- Beethoven's *Egmont* Overture
- Dukas: *The Sorcerer's Apprentice*
- Grieg: *Hall of the Mountain King*
- Holst: *The Planets Suite* (especially Mars)
- Khachaturian: *Spartacus*, the Adagio
- Mozart: Overture to *The Marriage of Figaro*
- Orff: 'O Fortuna', from *Carmina Burana*
- Ravel: *Bolero*
- Richard Strauss: *Also Sprach Zarathustra*
- Rossini: Overture to *The Thieving Magpie*
- Tchaikovsky: *1812 Overture*

- Vaughan Williams: *The Lark Ascending*
- Wagner: *Tannhäuser* Overture

THRILL-SEEKING

Thrill-seekers are generally *not* trying to kill themselves. The edge-technician, the danger-controller, is going for the CC. Anyone willing to freefall, sky-dive, fly, water-ski, leap or climb may achieve one: the surfer boring through the coil of a wave, the skier or speeding motorcyclist, senses forced against the wind, just on the knife-edge of control. Descending from one of four BASE jumps (the acronym stands for Building, Antenna, Span and Earth) gives you a CC that is like an out-of-body experience. Adrenalin junkies, as they are labelled by the uninitiated, are drawn to a place beyond fear, of catharsis, ego-release, timeless beauty and tranquillity.

Professional sport

Pro sport is a test of nerve, not simply of physical skill. The experiment pits skilled contestants against each other under time limits and constraints, motivated by shedloads of money. Millions of spectators can then watch as the nail-biting tension mounts. The Grand National commentary canters along, rises to a frantic crescendo as front-runners pass the post, and then tails off as they saunter into the winners' enclosure. This is the typical CC arc.

Television quizzes

TV quiz shows place contestants under a microscope as they ascend a ladder of questions. Reality shows expose contestants to gruelling emotional ordeals, exploring climaxing in the contestants and vicariously in the viewer.

Computer gaming

In computer games the CC is achieved with the help of a 'boss' – a computer-generated force that struggles with the player in a tense series of 'grades' and enables him to reach a final crisis.

THE ARTS

The arts are all predicated on tension and resolution. Usually, as in fiction, ballet, opera, cinema and theatre, this is delivered through a storyline that builds and takes the audience with it. But our great poems, paintings and sculptures also manifest it. The high point of a great work of art causes a fusion in the mind. The climax makes total sense. It is a visceral experience – the hairs rise on your arms. It takes the breath away. It may even have a 'cleansing' effect, coalescing and releasing confused or pent-up emotions and moving you to tears.

Theatre

Two millennia ago, Aristotle studied the effects of drama on theatre audiences. He noticed that the Greeks went through hell with the characters on stage, and the action built up to a moment of extreme tension before erupting in violence and terror. He divided a play into four parts:

- *protasis* – the showing of the characters
- *epistasis* – working up the plot and expectations
- *catastasis* – the climax of the play
- *catastrophe* – when all is unravelled, revealed and resolved.

The audience went away 'cleansed' of their emotions. Aristotle called what they had experienced *catharsis*. He was the first to use this expression.

Fiction

The central characters of great fiction are put through a wringer, and at the point of highest tension there is a supreme struggle, during which the protagonist fails or triumphs but dramatically learns. Writers explore extreme emotions, narrating their characters' crises and torments. They take their readers through these as well, in order to achieve a resolution. Perhaps the most famous example of a fictional epiphany comes from Charles Dickens. In *A Christmas Carol* hardened miser Scrooge is subjected to disturbing visions, the most harrowing concerning his own death. Scrooge is converted by all this terror into a joyous fellow who gives his money away and stands on his head.

Movies

All great movies, but scary movies particularly, carry the hallmarks of the CC art form, its patterns and devices. Alfred Hitchcock was known as the Master of Tension. His movies focused not on gore, but on unsettling the viewer. He wanted to 'make the audience suffer as much as possible'. The resolution, when it came, was so much more satisfying. Quentin Tarantino once boasted, 'We're gonna sell you this seat but you're only gonna use the edge of it.' Half the frightened movie-goer wants to escape, while the other half wants to know what happens. The climax and pay-off leave him flushed and laughing.

Classical music

Classical music transcends linguistic and cultural barriers and speaks directly to the brain. It has been composed by geniuses over the centuries to invoke the cerebral climax. Its complex notations are a formula, exquisitely developed, for producing tension and pressure in sounds and sequences, climbing, falling back and then climbing ever higher, to one CC after another. Listeners can both hear them and feel them.

> **Musical mind over matter**
> *Musical prodigy Lloyd Coleman was born in Bridgend, South Wales to working-class parents who knew nothing about classical music. He is deaf and almost blind, but at 17 he has taken the classical musical world by storm as a performer, composer and conductor. Lloyd is now being hailed as a second Beethoven, yet when doctors broke the news to his mother that her little boy was deaf as well as practically blind, she thought: 'What on earth is life going to hold for him now?' At seven years of age, Lloyd told her. He said, 'Mummy, my dream is to play in the Royal Albert Hall.' And he has – three times.*

GO ON – GIVE YOURSELF A THRILL!

If you are willing to try these arousal curve activities yourself, knowing what you now know, you will certainly see 'the shape of things that come'. Good luck, and enjoy! If anything is purpose-built to lift even the deepest gloom, it is the CC.

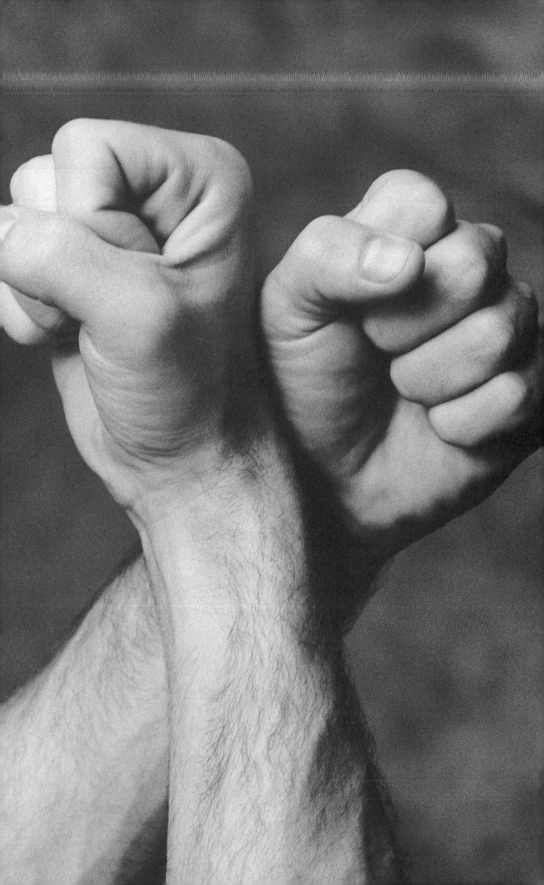

Getting tough

When I was agony aunt Marje Proops' official biographer back in the 1980s, it was part of my job to study her mail from troubled readers, over two million of whose letters were secretly housed in the *Daily Mirror* archives. A lot of the people who wrote to Marje were in despair because of the problems they faced, and most of them were frightened of someone or something.

Marje was renowned for her intelligent but very assertive brand of 'aunting', and often encouraged her readers to get tough – with themselves, their problems, their persecutors, or all of the above. They listened to Marje because they trusted her common sense, and time and again, as I could see from her correspondence, her robust advice 'did the trick'. More than once it literally saved people's lives.

Yet today when I offer very similar advice, I am accused of being a heartless bitch. This is because we are living now in an unusually protective, safety-conscious society that thinks the way to help the weak and vulnerable is to nurse them like infants and prevent them from feeling bad. But look at the number of adults who are suffering from depression and anxiety today and ask yourself: *Softly-softly – helping or harming?*

Have you ever wondered where the theory of 'stress management' actually came from? Past generations never even heard of it. Few people who believe in 'stress' trouble to look into its provenance. I have. Here is one *possible* interpretation of how it happened ...

DR JEKYLL AND MR HYDE REVISITED

Dr Jekyll is down on his luck. His latest experiments have been a bit controversial and his funding is up for review.

'Really, Hyde,' he says. *'I feel I'm wasting my time in that laboratory. I want something big.'*

'You want some big scare about people's 'ealf. Convince 'em they're about to drop dead or they're ready for the Rubber Ramada. Then you cures it, makes your pot, and retires to Brighton.'

'You mean something psychological – voodoo perhaps?'

'Voodoo could come into it, yerst. What you really want is a lurgie. You want people to have this lurgie, and then you turns round and cures it.'

'But, my good man, I can't invent a disease. You can't convince people they've got a disease if they haven't got a disease. They're going to want to see some symptoms.'

At this point, Mr Hyde becomes quite subdued. He scratches his very low forehead. Suddenly his ratty eyes brighten.

'What you do is, you pick something that the body does already, and you turn it into a disease! You say, "Them's yer symptoms!"'

'You mean like temperature? Every time somebody's temperature goes up, they have this condition?'

'Yerst. But you can do better than that.'

'Hmmmmm. There is actually a mechanism, Hyde, that people experience every day. A survival mechanism, the response to threat. It's not very pleasant either, so that would add to its charm, hwa hwa.*'*

''Assit, guvnor! You tell 'em every time they get that mechanism, they've got our disease. Then you just comes across with the cure.'

'But how would I cure a natural mechanism that's designed to galvanise them into action? I suppose I could tell them to calm down. That would dampen it

down a bit. But I'd need some kind of scientific backing – the medical community would never buy this.'

Hyde, deep in thought, runs his fingers through his face.

'I got it. I know how you get the scientific backing. You pay 'em. You pay some researchers. They'll prove whatever you tell 'em to prove.'

'Good lord, Hyde: you might be right. We could set up experiments using animals. They can't talk – you can prove whatever you like with them, and we could expose them to various tortures, which would inevitably have a bad effect on the little wretches. And then we could say this research proves that our lurgie is very dangerous, and every time people feel the signs, they had better look sharp and call us for help!'

'Well, what's the name of this here mechanism?'

'Actually it's called "the stress response".'

'Right. You could say you're "stress-doctoring", or "stress-boshing", summink like that, couldn't yer?'

'I like that. I do. Mr Hyde, I do believe I'm going to mix you a drink.'

And thus was created a monster!

LIFE SKILLS

So calling the natural response to threat by the medical-sounding name 'stress' makes people think that, every time they face a threat, they have this new disease. That sure would make life tough. But how *should* you equip someone with skills to enable them to handle life's problems? There are two key theories of emotional education, and they are opposites.

Theory one

The first theory, which we might call the 'stress management' method, is to offer protection and teach people to relax. Then when they meet life's crises, they will hopefully remain calm and not get upset. If possible the upsetting crises themselves must be avoided, or reduced by health and safety legislation, by social organisations and charities, by lawyers, by doctors using prescription medication, by employers, teachers and carers, and if all these fail, by government.

Theory two

The second method is to teach people coping skills and show them how to master their negative emotions by being exposed to hard training and challenges. Then they can deal with whatever life may throw at them – and it will throw a lot.

Where do you stand on these two?

Suppose you believe the first 'stress management' theory is right. Ask yourself this: how did past generations manage to cope with famine, plague, child mortality, imprisonment for debt, execution for beliefs, war, want and workhouses? Were they trained using the 'protective' approach? Of course not.

Whether you were

- a Roman

- a Spartan

- a bachelor knight

- an American Indian

- a Sumo wrestler

- an Australian settler

- an American prospector

- a Russian peasant

- a British 'Tommy'

- a London civilian during the Blitz

- an army or navy cadet

- a schoolchild

your training would have been most severe. The ideology behind it was based not on *avoiding* negative emotions, which would have struck our forebears as weird and unnatural, but on *rehearsing* them and thereby gaining mastery. All of our leisure pursuits, as well as rites of passage, are still based on this principle of going through fear, tension and tears, and then out the other side a little older and wiser, having possibly had a peak experience or self-discovery on the way.

MENTAL STRENGTH AND WEAKNESS

In all likelihood, what we call 'strength' and weakness' are not fixed personality traits at all. Whether we show courage or cower in the corner is a matter of choice. It depends on how much negative emotion we are prepared to put up with. Small children can know what it feels like to be a hero. This may explain why they occasionally jump off high walls, climb trees and eat worms (oh, yes). Decorated adult heroes may actually *feel* terror when they do what they do, as Susan Jeffers phrased it in her bestselling book, they *Feel the Fear and Do It Anyway*.[1] It is other people who perceive the strength or the weakness, not those who do the scary things.

Champion sportsmen may feel 'pressure' – unpleasant feelings of tension and fear at the height of competition – but steel themselves and go through the winning barrier anyhow. On the other hand also-rans experience the pressure, succumb to their fears, make mistakes and lose – even from supremely winning positions. In the sporting parlance they are said to have 'choked' or 'bottled it'. The difference is in the training: the harder and scarier the dress rehearsals, the tougher the competitor.

The Roman Army endured from 750 BC until the Siege of Constantinople in 1453. Its success was down to training. The legions' exercises, according to the historian Josephus, 'were like battles without the blood, so their battles were like exercises with blood'.

Winston Churchill's 'lion-hearted nation' (as the British were then called) referred to all this as 'character training' because it was meant to equip people with the spirit or *character* to cope with life's serious challenges. Call it unkind if you like, but in those days it was *do or die*. The good news is that, since we are all descended from those tough survivors, we should have in our genes some residue of that dour survival spirit and can all master coping skills if we are prepared to try.

'HARDENING'

The mechanism behind character-training is called inurement or hardening. How does it work? When you walk along the pavement by a busy road with fast cars and heavy lorries rumbling past your elbows, are you, as a rule, scared? Probably not. Because you have done it so many hundreds of times, the danger hardly registers. It is still there: a car could conceivably mount the footpath, but over time your brain has weighed up the statistics and decided that almost certainly nothing much will happen to you. When we are regularly and repeatedly exposed to a danger, our awareness of that danger reduces until we hardly notice it at all.

Examples of the *decreasing fear* curve:

- **Learning to drive**. On our first driving lesson, our knees may be knocking under the dashboard. Yet after lots of exposure at the wheel, we may end up falling asleep on the motorway because we are bored.

- **Watching a horror film**. When we watch a horror film for the first time, we may be shocked and scared. Yet if we see it again and again, we find the 'scares' dull and comical. The effect even happens across generations. Movies that frightened people half to death in the 1960s look pretty silly now.

- **Taming**. Laboratory animals may be timid during an initial experiment, and yet, exposed to the same stimulus again and again, they become progressively hardened to it and show little response. Researchers recognise 'taming' as a predictable effect. The word 'taming' is used to refer to any reducing response to stimuli.

NOW I'D LIKE YOU TO MEET ESMERALDA!

 How does one put this 'gradual reduction of fear' principle into practice? Well, supposing you were, let's say, *arachnophobic*. OK, I want you to imagine the biggest, blackest, longest-legged spider you could ever encounter. I know the one. She is called 'Esmeralda', she is made of metal, and she sits on my desk and sometimes in on my classes. Why?

When I moved to the country, I was paralysed with fear of spiders, even little ones. If I encountered an 'S' in my house, I had to phone for help. Late one night I was even reduced to shutting one in a bedroom and taping a warning notice on the door to remind me in the morning in case I wandered in there half asleep and had a heart attack.

Eventually I thought: *I cannot live like this. I've got to shape up.* Yes, I know there are desensitisation programmes and therapies on the market, but I wanted to help myself. So I had Esmeralda made by a metal sculptor, and I deliberately placed her in my line of sight every day while I was working. At first she scared the pants off me, but gradually I got used to her proportions. She was quite beautiful really. And these days, when even your economy-sized black bulbous arachnid scampers towards me I think, *Oh, look at that diddie*. I might, if I can be bothered, get a tumbler and card and chuck him or her outside. Problem solved.

I have loaned Esmeralda to trainees occasionally. She is a marvellous teaching assistant and costs little to run.

BRAIN TRAINING MADE EASY

Now, here is an intriguing idea for you to consider. What if the brain *rewarded* us for courage and *punished* us for cowardice? Surely that couldn't be true. Or could it? Consider these two scenarios.

The well-fed brain

Your brain consumes data, and it is hungry. It has a huge appetite for information and for electrochemically forging connections at its synapses that make sense of reality. We can surmise that it would therefore like you to go out and experience things, so that it can receive and store data about the world. This after all is what it was designed to do.

When we experiment, experience and say 'yes' to challenges, the brain 'rewards' us with highs and buzzes. Whether or not we succeed in our endeavours, we feel the benefit of showing courage because we get

- *an adrenalin rush beforehand*
- *exhilaration during and*
- *huge satisfaction after*

from having had the audacity to try. Even small children love dares. It brings a flush to their cheeks to put themselves in unusual, exciting and scary situations. They will challenge themselves whether you like it or not, and if you lock them in their bedrooms with only a computer for company, they will play dangerous games upon it!

The starved brain

The converse is also true. If we avoid experiences and quail from challenges, the brain 'punishes' us with fear. If we run from a situation, we become more leery and perceive it to be more terrifying at the next encounter. If we avoid it altogether, we may become frightened and anxious even in our hiding places. The brain is perhaps telling us: This is not normal. I need you to go out and let me process information about reality – otherwise how can I possibly learn? How can I make sense of the world if you do not let me at it?

Those who avoid life's thrills and spills end up afraid of life. Some can't even open their own front doors any more because of the volume of fear that has accumulated in their heads. The way for them to overcome that terror is gradually to increase their exposure to the world outside, so that their sense-starved brains can function normally again.

INSIDE THE BLACKENED ROOM

In the 1960s there was a surge of scientific interest in sensory deprivation. Volunteers were put in soundproof cubicles with no light and no other stimuli, to see how long they could last without any sensory input at all. Inside each SD room there was a panic button, and a lot of people used it. Their brains began to malfunction. They became terrified of nothing, even delusional.

From brains that are starved of stimuli, the feedback is confusion, insecurity and fear. This is why sensory deprivation has been used by ruthless regimes to brainwash solitary prisoners. It reduces them to cowering acceptance of any novel idea that might be presented to them by their captors, so hungry are their brains for a morsel of experience.

The motto is therefore:

> **Don't starve your brain or it may start acting peculiar.**
> **It could even turn on you and give you a fright!**
> **Feed it, exercise it regularly and you will keep it healthy and happy.**

NOTE

1. Susan Jeffers, *Feel the Fear and Do It Anyway*. Arrow edition, 1991.

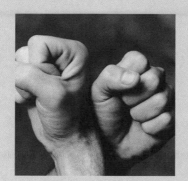

Meet the advisory panel

12

To assist me on this book, I have chosen a panel of ten 'expert advisers': people who either describe themselves right now as 'depressed' or who suffer periodically from despair. So meet my Team (I've changed their names to protect their identities).

THE TEAM

Maggie

I was in a psychiatric hospital for four months, and underwent psychotherapy and drug treatment. I still suffer from bouts of severe depression and I still take antidepressants, but I am willing to try some of the challenges, so long as you don't get on my case! I'm not very mobile.

Vaz

Losing my job in a leading broker's office robbed me of all my savings and self-esteem. I rowed with everybody. I have trouble staying awake in the daytime as I play the chat rooms and computer games, sometimes till daylight. We recently lost our nice house as I couldn't keep up the payments so we're in rented, a big comedown. I'm on benefit now and pretty much retired. How old am I? I'm 33.

Terry

This is all a bit artificial, but OK here goes: I lost my partner two years ago, after she had a miscarriage. I felt guilty as I wasn't that supportive, and it all fell apart, then I started getting down on myself. Like a lot of people I resorted to the bottle, but found it made me behave like a twat and I kept getting emotional, so now I avoid company. OK, I'll go for a challenge – nothing to lose.

Charlotte

I have various health problems, but I was diagnosed with body dysmorphia at a London clinic. I feel depressed because I just hate the way I look, and have been through anorexic episodes. If I could afford plastic surgery I think that would raise my self-confidence. I doubt very much that anything else will.

Katey

I have never had a proper job. I originally went for a singing career as I do have quite a good voice but got nowhere. My boyfriend left me because he says I am negative all the time and wouldn't do the gigs, but I got stressed out. I have had antidepressants including Prozac and before that Seroxat prescribed by my doctor, and I have tried counselling but didn't find that worked for me. Right, I've got nothing to lose by trying some challenges.

Philip

My main problem is apathy. I don't sleep much so I get up in the night to read or listen to local radio. Not one night – every night. I used to go to work with no sleep at all. I am usually tired anyway, but I feel defeated, as if I've had all the blood drained out of me. Some mornings I can't be bothered to get up at all, and the Job Centre have threatened to stop my benefit. That should scare me but it doesn't.

Susanna

I put on a lot of weight when I was looking after my Mum. I bought treats for her and when she wouldn't eat, I ate them myself. When Mum passed away I just went on eating. I feel like an old walrus, to be honest. Life has passed me by. Drugs? Yes, I have sertraline. Counselling? No, as I couldn't get on an NHS list.

George

I was made redundant after 25 years with the same firm. I've tried finding another job but the reaction you get is: oh – we're looking for someone young. That's if they bother to reply to your e-mails or letters at all. I feel as though I'm walking about invisible. Most of my friends were work-related and I don't see them as I can't afford to buy a round. I did part of the Restart course and found it helpful so would like to have a go at this.

Adrian

I've been what you're calling 'in despair' since I was at university, though I've been diagnosed as bi-polar. Yes, I've had counselling, also tranquillisers, antidepressants, you name it. No, I wasn't cured. I have wild manic episodes when I'm very creative and periods when I can't think as far as the next sentence. I am a philosophy tutor, and that makes you pry into the meaning of life, which is particularly not good if there isn't any.

Barbara

I divorced my husband after he had an affair with another woman. He was very undermining to me, criticising my dress, my hair, even the way I ate. On one occasion he left me at night in a supermarket car park and just drove off. I feel very down most of the time. I walk the dog, otherwise I don't go out.

I hope you can see where these people are coming from and can relate to at least some of their problems. They are all good sports and have been asked to try out the first nine Challenges (the tenth may take a while longer to complete), then choose the ones they found most beneficial and give us their feedback. As a couple of them have pointed out, they've really got nothing to lose by the exercise as they've tried practically everything else. One or two of them have already encountered the Heartless Bitch through training classes and know what to expect. For the rest, good luck, but you won't need it. Fortune really *does* favour the brave.

Part 2

Beating despair: the challenges

Now that you have been shown the theoretical basis of my psychological skills training we are going to turn to practicalities. During the following ten chapters I am going to set you ten challenges to vanquish despair. They are:

1 The Unblocker (and warm-up)
2 The Fitness Challenge
3 The Task Challenge
4 The Social Challenge
5 The Mood Change Challenge
6 The Nature Challenge
7 The Performance Challenge
8 The Creative Challenge
9 The Fear Challenge
10 The Life Challenge

All of the challenges are based on my Colchester Restart training course for the long-term unemployed, which had not only the best record in the region, but a better outcomes record than all the other training providers combined. With the help of a wonderful recruitment boss in Jo Moore, whose company it was, the Mojo course got people back to work who had never worked in their lives, who had languished on the dole since coming out of school or prison, and who had serious social and psychological problems including depression, Asperger's syndrome, claustrophobia, resignation, helplessness, severe social handicaps, homelessness, violence, debt, bereavement, divorce and rock-bottom confidence.

Each module of the course consisted of a seven-hour training day. The training offered practical advice and evidence-based techniques for improving emotional skills, tackling mental barriers, changing negative attitudes and addressing fears. Each one was carefully devised under supervision as it had to be proven to be of practical use to the long-term unemployed and help them with their hang-ups and mental health issues. It was funded by the government through the Employment Service.

The training covered a wide spectrum of psychological skills, from simple but effective problem-solving techniques to overcoming rejection, from understanding 'nerves' to motivation, and from improvisation to brain power techniques. The training placed great emphasis on creativity, on inspiration, on identifying and using latent talents. And it explored and explained the nature of peak experiences and the arousal curve, emotional competence in crises and brilliance.

The following challenge programme has been designed to support and encourage – that is 'to give courage to' – the depressed or helpless reader who would like to get back into the driving seat and take command of life. It does not mollycoddle and some of the challenges may appear quite daunting, at least initially. But each is carefully explained in detail beforehand, and each is based on sound research and common sense.

The tasks recommended may be tackled by anyone of any age and are designed to be taken at your own pace. You may wish to involve friends and colleagues, but the challenge programme is ultimately something you must undertake yourself. It is not enough for a self-help book like this to explain the thinking and the research behind a life-changing programme. In order to be of any real use to someone in despair, it must also provide a practical stairway out of hell. This is that stairway. Take the ten steps and you will reach a better place.

One: the unblocker challenge

This series of ten challenges is designed to change your ways. If you are in despair, clearly *your ways need to change.* How do you spend your days at the moment? Chances are your days are currently spending *you*. Let's try an experiment. Below is a week time grid. Fill it in as honestly as you can. There are 168 hours in your week. Distinguish between paid work (£WORK) and unpaid work (NON£WORK), as, for example, working in a charity shop or doing your accounts or writing up projects to try to generate income. 'TICKOVER' means general maintenance, e.g. grooming the home, the garden or yourself, shopping, ironing, etc.

MY CURRENT WEEK

HOURS (out of 168)	SLEEP	SOCIAL	£WORK	TICK-OVER	NON £WORK	STUDY	OTHER
80							
60							
40							
30							
20							
10							
0							

When you have filled your grid, sit back and look at it. Is that how you want to spend the rest of your days? This is not a dress rehearsal. This is your life. That clock applies to you. It is telling your time. On our Restart courses, many of the candidates found they spent an inordinate amount of hours in bed. Their 'sleeping sickness' was both a symptom and a cause of their malaise. I would recommend a loud alarm clock – and a pin within easy reach next to it in case they still couldn't rouse themselves. A lot of candidates found they were filling the 'OTHER' column with hours spent playing computer games or watching television and DVDs. Nothing wrong with leisure activities; something wrong with disappearing into screens and monitors for most of the week. So what I would ask *you* to do now is to fill in another identical grid, but this time re-allocating your hours *the way you would like them to be*. See what happens when you do this.

MY REVISED WEEK

HOURS (out of 168)	SLEEP	SOCIAL	£WORK	TICK-OVER	NON £WORK	STUDY	OTHER
80							
60							
40							
30							
20							
10							
0							

When you have had the chance to consider the difference, ask yourself – *Why am I wasting so much of my time right now?* As the Ancient Romans said, *time flies*. Once it is gone you never, ever, get it back. And if your response to *that* is, 'I really don't care, as there's nothing I want to do any more,' then the following challenge is designed especially for you.

A SENSE OF WONDER

What can give you back your sense of wonder? A child has only to look out of the window to see something magical, but we lose the gift as we get older and our vision is dulled by life's troubles. The magic is still really there, but how do we retrieve it? William Wordsworth said in his famous poem 'Ode: Intimations of Immortality':

> Our birth is but a sleep and a forgetting:
> The Soul that rises with us, our life's Star,
> Hath had elsewhere its setting,
> And cometh from afar:
> Not in entire forgetfulness,
> And not in utter nakedness,
> But trailing clouds of glory do we come
> From God, who is our home:
> Heaven lies about us in our infancy!
> Shades of the prison house begin to close
> Upon the growing boy,
> But he beholds the light, and whence it flows,
> He sees it in his joy ...

So in this first challenge we are going to try to recapture your childhood sense of 'seeing things anew'. You will also be taking one small step towards helping yourself. But *before* you attempt to take any action, we are going to 'warm you up' with some improvisation. The reason is simple: if you just went ahead and tried the small assignment in the usual way, your mind would probably be cluttered with past failures, doubts about self-confidence and queries about the meaning of the task (or the meaning of life). Trust me: you either wouldn't do it or you wouldn't do it with any enjoyment or panache. Thinking on your feet, though, 'frees the soul'. It allows adults to recapture the imaginative thinking of childhood. There is magic in improvisation exercises, and they transformed my often *very* depressed and demoralised trainees, no matter what wicked witch had allegedly stolen their sparkle.

WHY DO PEOPLE JUST SIT THERE?

When people get into this habit of just sitting there, it's not through a lack of intelligence. It's not because they are not thinking. Often they are thinking *too much*. Do you know the story of the Imprisoned Butterfly? When he was a little caterpillar he had to forage. He didn't think about it. He just went out and climbed on stuff and ate stuff. Then the time came to pupate, and because he suddenly had time to think about what he was doing, and what it meant to have wings, and what it might be like to crash into a wall – he got stuck.

Right – now try this.

> **Written exercise**
>
> *We've all got things that we think we can't do. Write down at least one thing (or possibly two or three things) you can't do that you think you ought to be able to do. Take five minutes of your precious life to write them down. Don't show them to anybody.*

We will come back to them later as they are important. But right now, look at that list. You can do those. What's stopping you? Nothing. Make every excuse, blame other people, blame circumstances, blame it on money. It's not those things. What's stopping you? One word – *you*. It's you! You have a brain. Your brain is just as big and data-rich and impressive as anybody else's, as anybody's that you admire, as anybody's who has changed the world. You can, you really can. It's not just words. It's not just 'positive thinking'. You *can*. All you have to do is *Stop stopping you*. 'But *HOW*? How can I stop stopping me?' you say. 'I get so depressed!'

I've been down there at the bottom of the well, just like you. That's why I want you to succeed and I am determined that you will. In this book I offer you the benefit of 25 years' research on the works and wonders of the human brain. In fact I'm not talking to *you* at all – I'm talking to your brain! I want it to get a wake-up call. I will do whatever it takes to turn it back on again and jump you out of the deadness, so you can 'behold the light and whence it flows' as you used to do.

IMPROVISATION

I am going to give you some improvisation exercises. When you see what they are, I don't want you to start second-guessing and putting up cynical barriers. 'I'm not really going to try. I'm not engaging in the exercises. I'm going to do them in a half-hearted way, as if they're beneath my dignity, or as if I can't be bothered. That way I won't make a fool of myself.' This would ensure one thing – the experiment won't work. Let's overcome the deadness. Improvisation is designed to get behind the facade we regularly show the world.

Some of the exercises come from an inspirational theatre director called Keith Johnstone. Years ago I used to interview famous actors, and one or two of them mentioned this marvellous book they had read called *Impro*.[1] It is chock full of wonders. For a start Johnstone claims that education has meant the elimination of fantasy, because kids are corrected for coming out with 'the wrong thing'. He also suggests that what we call 'self-expression' is really a misconception. The Inuit believes a piece of bone contains one figure only, and that by selflessly carving away a sculptor can find it.

Johnstone says that uncreative people are ashamed of the 'madness' of creators. We are taught that the first thing that comes to mind is 'psychotic, obscene, unoriginal or inappropriate'. He explains: 'We suppress our spontaneous impulses, we censor our imaginations, we learn to present ourselves as ordinary – and we destroy our talent – then no one will laugh at us.' When actors came to him for training, a lot of them were just showing off. Most were wooden. Despite long efforts in rehearsals and practice and talking and pep-talking to get the wooden ones to act, they still couldn't do it. They were stiff and scared as they 'tried' to be natural. So to allow his actors to escape their prisons of self-consciousness, Johnstone collected 'impro' exercises. They helped his actors. They helped my unemployed trainees. I think they will help you.

RULES FOR IMPROVISING

The more obvious you are, the more natural you will appear. If you try to think up 'original' things, you will seem mediocre. Be obvious. Accept the first word that comes into your head. What your imagination comes up with is not your fault. It may come from afar! The following exercise is one that you can try out on a friend, just to demonstrate how the thing works.

GUESSING A STORY – Exercise with a friend

A invents a story by letting B 'guess' what it's about.

A – You don't have to know a story. Just tell B this is a story about ... (any subject that springs to mind). B must then guess the story by asking you questions. You answer 'no' if their question ends with a vowel, 'yes' if it ends in a consonant and 'maybe' if it ends in a 'y'. If they start getting discouraged answer with more 'yesses'. The results may amaze you ...

All impro work is based on making connections – fast and without thinking. Since Donald Hebb came up with the idea in 1945 scientists have known that the brain works by *making connections across its synapses*. This is what it likes to do. And this is really what 'creativity' is all about. Try these:

CONNECTIONS – Exercise 1

Ask somebody to call out three different objects. Your task is very quickly and without thinking to combine them, out loud, in a story. Don't try to be 'funny' or 'original'. Just let your imagination have its say.

CONNECTIONS – Exercise 2

*If you are stuck in traffic, look at the car registration plate in front. Make up a story or a piece of nonsense loosely based on the letters and numbers. **NI80 EHE** might give you 'Norman had 18 Operations. Enemas Had Encouraged them'. Or you could use postcodes, e.g. **C28 1UF** might come out as 'Cyril's lucky number was 28, but 1 day it Undid his Fortunes'.*

CONNECTIONS – Exercise 3

Take a newspaper and without thinking or planning, make dots on three words randomly chosen in the printed text. Connect them up in a storyline. Cheating or picking out 'matching' words will defeat the object.

Now try these improvisation exercises to 'warm you up' for self-help action.

DRAWING WITH BOTH HANDS – Improvisation exercise 1

Take a piece of paper and two pens (felt tips are good). Now without thinking or trying to be 'artistic', draw a house or a face. Don't switch your gaze from one hand to the other: it's better if you stare somewhere in between. It's an odd sensation but see what you get.

PERIPHERAL VISION – Improvisation exercise 2

Notice something in the corner of your vision. Don't look at it: just be aware of it. Keep it in mind for a few moments without being tempted to look.

Now look at it. What do you notice? It appears sharper.

WRONG NAMES – Improvisation exercise 3

Go round the room and shout out the wrong name for everything your eyes light on. Now stop and look at your shoes. Do they look different? How?

THE UNBLOCKER

While these exercises are *still fresh in your mind*, you are going to (choose one of the following):

- **make a key phone call**

- **send an important e-mail**

- **make a significant appointment (e.g. bank manager, dentist, Citizens Advice Bureau)**

- **arrange to meet somebody who can affect your life**

- **ask somebody who can help you to help you**

- **sign on for a class or a course**

- **book into a gym, a Pilates class, a Weight Watchers class, etc.**

- **send for a college prospectus, etc.**

If there is an interval between the exercises and the action, refresh your imagination by *repeating* the improvisations as a warm-up before you start. Remember: don't ponder the pros and the cons. Do like the seal: *Just jump in.*

Reprise your 'I can't' exercise

Remember that exercise you did at the beginning, when you wrote down the thing or things you couldn't do that you felt you ought to be able to do? Look at them again. Now very quickly brainstorm some ideas on how you could do them. Write the answers down on a piece of paper.

WHAT PANEL MEMBERS THOUGHT

Maggie

'I was reluctant to do the exercises as they seemed a bit childish but then I thought: what the hell? The one that really worked for me was drawing with both hands – I drew a lousy house with a bent chimney, but afterwards it felt odd, as if I'd had a tot! Then I made my call, not the bank manager or anything, only my sister-in-law. But I hadn't spoken to her in nearly five years as we'd had a disagreement, and we just started chatting as though nothing had happened. I didn't tell her what I'd just been doing. She has been diagnosed with depression. It was rather strange.'

George

'I remember when we did these in Restart and we were all shouting out the answers. OK, I haven't been keeping them up since, but I did do the connections ones and the Peripheral Vision one as I had a job interview. I don't know the result yet but I tell you what – I wasn't nervous. I kept making the bloke laugh.'

Barbara

'The self-help thing I chose was to make an appointment to have my hearing tested. I've been having the telly on loud lately and I didn't like to say anything. The exercises did cheer me up actually. I couldn't do the drawing one, but the one looking out of the corner of your eye was good, and the wrong names for the furniture one. So maybe they helped, you never know.'

Katey

'I thought they were brilliant, especially the wrong names and guessing the story. I did them with my mate Lisa and we fell about. I didn't want to do any of the tasks though as I couldn't think of one, but just to keep the faith I sent for an am-dram thing off the Internet I could have a go at – probably won't.'

Terry

'They didn't work for me but I did send a couple of e-mails. One was to my old IT boss. When he called me back I asked him to give me a job and he said no. Sod you, I said, and he laughed. I haven't spoken to him in a while. He used to have some good contacts. To be fair I think the exercises would work for a lot of people with depression because they use a different pathway in your brain.'

NOTE

1. Keith Johnstone, *Impro: Improvisation and the Theatre*. Faber & Faber, 1979, p. 84.

Two: the fitness challenge

When was the last time you walked in a field or down a towpath or by a lake? Even if you live in the centre of a town, there are green spaces and parks and trees somewhere not far away. Go and find one. When Beethoven was in utter despair because he was losing his hearing, he used to stride about on his own in the countryside with his arms behind his back. It made him feel renewed. You can hear it in his music.

NATURE AND DESPAIR

Some of the earliest mental *asylums* (meaning sanctuaries) were set in large rural grounds in which patients were expected to work the vegetable and flower plots. Horticulture was seen as a wholesome therapy for the mentally ill, and these asylum grounds inspired all the hospital gardens that flourished until the middle of the twentieth century, when they were gradually replaced by drug and 'talking' cures. Now horticultural therapy is enjoying a comeback in Britain and the US, with initiatives underway like the Natural Growth Project in Hampstead, which helps the victims of torture, and patients' gardens at Bethlam Hospital near Beckenham in Kent and the Blackthorn Medical Centre, Maidstone. The gardens make people who are full of pain feel better.

Nature can heal. You often see a little plaque on somebody's lawn that reads: *You are nearer to God in a garden than anywhere else on earth*. So even if you have to get there with help because you are in a wheelchair, I want you to go somewhere you can see trees or open spaces and just *breathe*. This is air that doesn't come from central heating systems or exhaust pipes. Look around. Nature is bigger than you, and it is cyclical. Renewal goes on uninterrupted, whether you choose to take part in it or not. It doesn't depend on human perception. If you are in despair, you need to understand that you are a part of this natural rhythmic process. You belong here. Start giving it some time.

Depressed by pain

If you are in despair because you suffer from chronic pain, this Challenge may be especially relevant to you. Close contact with nature is both refreshing and rejuvenating. If you are in constant pain that 'gets you down' it is very important that you do not just submit to it, as this will increase your experience of the pain. You need to look outwards, not just inwards.

You can moderate your pain levels by choosing to help yourself and gain mastery over your moods and your activities. Many physiotherapists teach that 'motion is lotion' and that lying in bed with a bad back, for example, can cause the muscles to contract and the pain to increase. The less you move, the more your joints may stiffen and the more they stiffen, the more you hurt.

Conversely, the brain can release natural opiate-like substances, and when we are totally absorbed in an activity we often do not notice our pain at all. I have seen professional sportsmen quite badly injured come off the field completely unaware that they have damaged themselves because they were so alive playing their sport.

THE DIRTY WORD

Now, **fitness**, for some despairing people, is a dirty word. They have escaped from the subject for so long they think it might hurt them to turn round and look at it. So let me tell you a story to give you hope.

Valentin's story

When Russian circus performer Valentin Dikul was 24, he fell off a trapeze after a cable snapped. He was rushed to hospital where doctors told him that the injury had severed his spinal cord. He would be paralysed from the waist down for the rest of his life. He would certainly never walk again.

Valentin lay in bed grieving and thinking. He asked a friend to bring some weights in and began to exercise his arms. The nursing staff smiled to see the poor man wasting his time. His back was broken. He must make the adjustment and accept it.

Valentin did not accept it. He exercised all the parts of his body that would move, and then, still working with weights, began a plan to get his brain to redirect nerve signals to strengthen his wasted legs, and even – what everybody said was impossible – to move them. Some of the nerves might still be connected. His exercise regime was gruelling, but it was his passion. He wanted to walk and he would walk. Today Valentin walks. He also works. And he is very, very strong. Now 70, he has opened clinics in France, Italy, Japan and Poland to help rehabilitate people with serious back injuries. He has had 136,000 applications for his treatment from around the world.

You may not have to go as far as Valentin. Take stock of your present state of fitness. Where are you on this list?

● I am in a wheelchair.

● I can walk with a stick.

● I can walk but with difficulty.

● I can walk.

● I can walk fast.

● I can jog.

● I can run.

If you are in a wheelchair, ask someone to help you get out into the fresh air to look at trees or a garden or fields *at least* once or twice a week. No matter what you have to do to insist upon it, and no matter what the season, make sure this happens to you. *You have a natural right to Nature.* You can also help yourself by doing what I call 'bed callisthenics'.

Bed callisthenics

This means that you lie in bed or on a couch and, starting with your feet and ankles, stretch, tense and relax each of your muscles in turn. You can increase the tension by using, for example, your left leg to press against your right leg, your left hand and arm to press against your right, and so on. If you make a 'praying hands' shape, you can work your arms and fingers quite effectively. Try what you can do without hurting yourself. By strengthening your muscles you can gradually reduce both your pain and your helplessness.

If you can walk with difficulty, use all your powers of persuasion to get assistance and get out there in a green space, moving about. It will make *such* a difference to your health and well-being that it will be worth the effort. Of course, for anyone who *is* able to walk, let alone run, there is simply no excuse. Move your behind out to Nature so she can heal your mind. Walk regularly:

- beginning once a week

- then twice a week

- then three times a week

- then every day

- ten minutes good

- twenty minutes better

half an hour or more, absolutely beautiful.

If you have legs that work, use them. Otherwise Valentin would be utterly ashamed of you. Once you are actually moving about, we can be more ambitious. We can talk about big words like these that will require you to ask your doctor's advice *before* you embark on them:

GYM

SWIM

SLIM

GYM

When we come to the fear challenge we shall be exploring adventure activities. If you want to try these – and I hope you will – you may need to advance your level of fitness beyond the baseline we are establishing here. Joining a gym is an ideal way of doing this because once you have paid your subscription fees, all you have to do is *turn up*. Even if you feel lousy when you arrive, you will soon be swept along by the atmosphere and the motivated people there. It may hurt a bit, but before you know it the sessions are over anyway. If you are lazy like me, going to a gym simplifies self-discipline. Because it places you in a fitness zone, you will get on and do the actions required, and the glow of pride you get from working out will encourage you to go back. If you can't afford a gym, try a fitness video, but *ask your doctor first*.

SWIM

If you are disabled or injured, your base level of fitness doesn't *have* to be low at all. Go on the website of the *Battle Back* organisation and look at those terribly wounded soldiers getting flushed doing their downhill racing and adventure activities. Watch the Paralympians strutting their stuff, with the sheen of sweat glistening on their foreheads and their heads held high with pride. If you are disabled or injured and your base level *is* low, the best way to move yourself may be swimming. If you can get to a pool, hydrotherapy is a most gentle and thorough way of exercising because it places no stress (in the engineering sense) on your joints. Do it regularly and watch the difference both in your fitness and your moods.

SLIM

Comfort eaters

Depressed people tend to 'comfort eat'. They also pour toxic liquids down their throats that depress their central nervous systems and make them act stupidly. A lot of them suck nicotine delivery devices. So comfort-eaters get overweight, unfit and slouchy, feel half asleep half the time and look like death warmed over. This feeds into their despair. How to break this vicious cycle?

Kind foods and cruel foods

This is really 'slimming made easy'. I'm not going to ask you to go on a diet. Diets tend to be too technical and complex for depressed people to handle. They get discouraged, give up and feel even worse than they did before they started. So I'm just going to explain a very simple new way of looking at what you eat and drink. It is so simple that when you prepare meals you can easily remember it, and when you shop it will make choosing foods child's play. If you are responsible for feeding other people, you will have it shining there in your head like a little beacon. This is it.

Kind foods

Kind foods are low in fat (less than 3%), low in sugar and low in salt. Kind foods are very good for depressed people because they treat your body with respect. After you've eaten them they reward you and support you and give you the energy to face life. If you suffer from despair, kind foods will steadily build up your reserves of energy and fitness, and help your brain marshal its powers to help you. Kind foods will make you stronger and slimmer. They will give you back your self-respect and confidence. Kind foods include lots of fresh fruit and vegetables, wholegrain cereals and pulses and are natural and easy to prepare. You can find recipes anywhere to make them delicious as well as nourishing, so long as you don't cover them with fat when you are cooking and turn them into something else.

Cruel foods

Cruel foods are high in fat, sugar or salt. They seem gorgeous and adorable when you are eating them but once they get inside you, they betray you and hurt you like a soap opera love-rat. They promise you comfort only to deceive you and bring you down. After you've had them – or rather they've had you – you feel fat, low and lousy.

Cruel foods don't fulfil their delicious promise. That's just a front. They really mean to destroy you. If you are in despair, you are especially vulnerable to cruel foods and their evil charms. Yes, they give you a little lift, but only so that they can bring you down after you've let them into your body. They've hurt you so many times before, yet you haven't realised what they are. They seem so nice at the time, but leave you feeling guilty and miserable. If you give cruel foods to those you love, just watch them swell up in front of you and start behaving badly. They can't help it. You've given them cruel foods. Kings used to have 'tasters' that tried their food first in case somebody was trying to poison them. Your family doesn't have a taster. They have you.

Cigarettes and alcohol are cruel too. You think you're sucking them, but really they are sucking you. They interfere with your brain so it finds it difficult to work for you. They are literally chemical depressants, promising highs and delivering lows. What else would you call such things, other than cruel?

SLOWLY DOES IT

You won't be able to change from cruel foods to kind foods overnight, but one by one I want you to start switching from a cruel food to a kind one. Introduce more kind foods into your diet and look for them when you shop. Cruel foods are everywhere in the supermarket and at the checkout, and every time you resist one, it says sucks to them all, and cheers to you. Gradually switching is the easiest way. The change in your moods, your health and your looks will also be gradual – this isn't a case of 'one leap and he was free'. But slowly and surely you will feel fitter, stronger, healthier and less depressed. Take the fitness challenge. Walk, flex and stretch, and switch foods. Try it – you'll like it.

WHAT PANEL MEMBERS THOUGHT

Vaz

'This interests me because I've always mixed with a lot of fairly unhealthy people at work and it makes sense that I let myself skid. Look, I've even bought a pair of trainers! I don't mind walking as I can still talk on the phone. Shit, I'm only 33 – a lot of people are a lot older than that and manage to drag themselves out, don't they. I thought the advice about food was a bit girlie but OK, if that's what it takes.'

Maggie

'I find it quite difficult to walk as I get out of breath, but I know exactly what you mean. When I can get out in a field or a forest somewhere, I do feel so very much better inside. I'm aiming to try this challenge as soon as I'm physically able to. The diet advice I think is absolutely true and absolutely right.'

Susanna

'This chapter was written for me! I love the "Kind and Cruel Food" idea. If you think about it, this is what they are doing to your body. They make you fat so you get more depressed. I've actually stopped myself buying the automatic bag of treats. If I don't stuff them they can't stuff me. I want to look better than this. The walking is really a struggle, but when you come back things don't look quite so bad. Ten minutes is my lot at the moment, but it's a start.'

Philip

'The last thing I want to do after a sleepless night is go for a walk, but when I did, I felt less tired rather than more tired. They say it helps you sleep, so I'll probably keep going with this.'

Three: the task challenge

Which of the following do you think will be more likely to raise your morale?

1 Finding the courage to face up to problems.
2 Hiding in the airing cupboard.

If you think maybe the first, this chapter is for you. The task challenge is designed to turn you around to face the front. Without necessarily realising it, you may not be facing forwards at the moment. You may be trying to recapture your lost youth. You may be trying to regress to a past life as an Indian chieftain. You may even *be* hiding in the airing cupboard. So let's start with some simple, practical strategies to help you.

Some psychologists think that you shouldn't call problems 'problems': you should call them 'projects'. I prefer to call a spade 'a spade'. We are not doing semantic exercises here: we are changing lives. And right now you may imagine that your problems are worse than anybody else's problems. A lot of depressed people do, and this is why they are depressed. So try this.

PROBLEM-SOLVING GRIDS

Take a blank sheet and divide it into three columns (or you can use the grid I've drawn up for you overleaf). Head one column 'M' for Moderate and the second column 'S' for Serious. List your problems in one column or the other, according to how you perceive them. Yes, of course it's subjective – your perception is crucially important. For each moderate problem score 1 and for each serious problem score 3. In the last column, if you already *know* the solution or adjustment (some problems like 'ageing' have no solution, but require an adjustment) you score *minus* 1 on that row. Fill in the grid as honestly as you can, and then total your problem quota at the bottom. If you do the exercise again next week, your score may well change. My trainees did this exercise with remarkable results.

PROBLEM QUOTA

M	S	SOLUTIONS/ ADJUSTMENTS

SCORING

You score 1 point for every M and 3 points for every S. If you *know* the solution/adjustment to your problem, deduct 1 point for each solution.

MY PROBLEM QUOTA (this week anyway) is ....

When the results were read out, those carrying the highest scores were not necessarily those who were depressed or felt they could not cope or 'face life any more'. Some people scored high on what they admitted were relatively modest problems that worried them unduly, simply because they could not (or in some cases would not) cope with them. On the other hand, 'survivors' with good coping skills who were grappling with major problems like homelessness, huge debts and bereavement felt that they could manage and problem-solve *even though* their scores were high.

Strangest of all, some who scored low were actually people in despair who preferred not to think about their problems at all. Because they never addressed or admitted their problems, they had no idea how to solve them. They also had a vague sense of anxiety and dread that things were somehow out of control and that the best solution was to bury their heads in the sand.

They were incorrect.

Setting out your problems in grids helps you to *externalise* and *organise* your thoughts. You can examine problems this way and keep a note of progress. It also gives you a sense of proportion.

Another problem-solving exercise: draw a 7 × 8 grid or use the one overleaf. Enter your problems one by one in the boxes along the top. If you have lots more than seven, just make the grid bigger. Use your initiative! Then down the side, list each action you are taking to try to solve that particular problem. Add to the Action list over time until you find the one that works. That Problem column then ends. You can add any new ones that occur to you.

PROBLEM-SOLVING GRID

Problem							
Action 1							
Action 2							
Action 3							
Action 4							
Action 5							
Action 6							
Action 7							
Action 8 *etc.*							

'BRAINSTORMING'

Brainstorming can offer you a fresh style of problem-solving by accessing parts of your brain that you may not normally use for this purpose. First, warm up using the following game. It may take a while, but we need to demonstrate to your satisfaction one of your brain's many under-used skills. Take a road map or an atlas or an A to Z. *Don't open it yet.* Write down from memory :

- a dozen places ending in *-mouth*

- a dozen places ending in *-borough*

- a dozen places containing *-ness* (this *is* hard).

Really try to remember *without* cheating, and when you run out of options, leave it for a while and go and do something *else*. At first you may keep worrying away at the problem, trying hard to recall the missing place names and failing. Stop. Just leave it. Make a cup of tea, or water the garden or something. Then, as you do these *other* tasks, a mysterious thing will generally happen. Odd place names will start to pop into your head. Jot them down when they come unbidden. Then, when you have a few, go and look for them in the map index. One or two may not actually exist, or they may be slightly inaccurate versions of real place names. But some of them will be exactly right – place names that you have seen on your travels but that you didn't know you knew, and that you certainly didn't remember on the first 'trawl'. What's happening is that your brain is presenting you with raw data. It is in its unedited form, like uncut diamonds. It is up to you to make use of this data by verifying or adapting it to suit your purposes. This is how 'brainstorming' works.

Now brainstorm a real problem

While the place-name exercise is still fresh in your mind, brainstorm one of the problems on your grids. Write down any solutions that occur to you, even inchoate and apparently absurd ones. Weird as they may first appear, perhaps they make 'imaginative' sense rather than logical sense, and perhaps therefore you can use them.

Once you have mastered the grids and the brainstorming, we can move on to the more exciting business of 'Facing the Monster'.

'OH-NO' TASKS

Choosing to tackle something you normally like to put off will demonstrate the before-and-after effects of 'Facing the Monster' – a principle that was the key to success for so many of my trainees. Finally tackling an onerous chore generally demonstrates two things: one, it wasn't as bad as your vivid imagination suggested, and two, it gives you a real buzz when you finish. These 'oh-no' tasks may not necessarily be that important in themselves, but they are important if they have been avoided and therefore have assumed an aura of 'cannot do'.

Examples of 'oh-no' tasks:

- Clearing a cupboard

- Organising your papers

- Going to see a dentist

- Sorting out finances

- Seeing the bank manager

- Having an eye-test

- Breaking bad news

- Doing self-assessment tax returns

- Asking for a pay rise or time off

- Sorting out a mess

- Asking for somebody's help

- Turning somebody down

- Expressing your true feelings

There are plenty more: life is peppered with them. If only we never had to do any of these, we'd all be awfully jolly all the time. But then we would not make remarkable discoveries about our abilities either. Now I want you to make your own list like this:

My 'oh-no' list

1 ....
2 ....
3 ....
4 ....
5 ....
6 ....
7 ....
8 ....

If you have more than eight 'oh-no' tasks I suggest your need for this exercise is *very great* and that you should therefore do it with alacrity. Now choose one task that you have been putting off for a *long* time. Why haven't you done it yet? Look at it. You can tackle that. You really *want* to tackle it because continually putting it off makes you feel sick inside. It also makes you feel like a wimp. You are *not* a wimp, and you are not going to act like a wimp. So now take the following action. Yes, you may be nervous. Do it anyway.

1 **Write down what you feel before you tackle the task (apprehensive, angry, frustrated, annoyed, nervous, scared, etc.).**
2 **Pay particular attention to *the moment you decide to go ahead.***
3 **Notice how you may get 'a rush of blood' as your brain takes command and sets to work on it.**

After you have tackled the task, sit down and consider what you feel *now*. I can assure you from my training work, my research and my own personal experience that a warm glow of satisfaction is virtually guaranteed. You won't just have got one particularly odious job out of the way – it is more than that. You will be inwardly rewarded. You will feel positive, concentrated, constructive and creative, because you have given your brain the chance to do what it loves best and what it was designed for – *helping you to survive.*

The brain is a servo-mechanism. It waits for your instructions. When these are received the effect is often palpable. You feel a thrill, a lift. And, in exactly the same way, you can summon your brain to help you with *all* your problems. It is there like a genie in a bottle, just waiting for you to ask.

Go ahead – face the monster!

WHAT PANEL MEMBERS THOUGHT
Katey
'I have a hell of a lot of "oh-no" tasks because I find that taking antidepressants and tranquillisers can make you a bit of a Mexican – you know: "*Manyana, manyana* – I'll do it tomorrow" ... The brainstorming with the map book was freaky. On the automatic remembering I got "Knarlsborough" and "Crowborough" that I'd never even *heard* of, and I also got "*Desperough*". I thought I must definitely have made that one up, but then when I looked there really *is* a Desborough. Your brain knows more than you think. The problem I wanted to face was about our drop-in closing down as that really causes problems for me. For that one I put: "Radio Essex". No reason. But then I picked up the phone and rang their helpline. I got my views

across and people heard it. How weird is that. It gives you a boost to do stuff you don't do.'

Barbara

'This whole "face the monster" idea is something I will carry with me. I face each wave now head-on. You've got to – it's no good running away as that doesn't solve anything. I've tackled a particular problem in that I'd lost a lot of friends after my divorce and I haven't had much of a social life. So my challenge was to get myself on two evening classes: I'm learning French and I'm doing fashion sewing and meeting some nice people. I wouldn't have done that if it hadn't been for the head-on challenge.'

Terry

'When you said I had to do this I thought: you have *got* to be joking. My no-can-do was to call my ex about selling our house because of the mortgage arrears. She's with somebody else now and we're talking legal and **** knows what and I was bricking it. Every time I thought of doing it I would find some reason [not to], making out I'd do it this evening, or do it when I was down the pub. Anyway this went *on* and *on*. I worked out choice remarks etc., but I still wasn't doing it. The exercises with the grids and the maps annoyed me to be honest – I thought – What the **** is this all about? I've got a Satnav anyway. But OK I made the call. Job done. I never made the tasty remarks, just talked normally. Bit of an anti-climax really. She was cool with it. I never even had a drink! When you actually get on and do it, you wonder what all the fuss was about. I knew that myself in fact, but if I'm totally honest I've been ducking things, socially and otherwise. There are calls I won't make and buff envelopes I won't open. I'm not saying I'm a hero now or anything but I reckon if I can do that, I can do other things.'

Four: the social challenge

16

Talking to a stranger or making a cold call to discuss a work project are the sorts of social challenge that many people, especially depressed people, believe they 'cannot do'. Except that of course they can. These are some of the most popular excuses people use to prevent themselves from doing social challenges:

- I'm nervous.

- I'm not confident.

- I might say the wrong thing.

- I'm no good with people.

- I wouldn't know where to start.

- They may not like me.

- I could make an idiot of myself.

NERVOUSNESS

So you get nervous. So what? In an earlier chapter we looked at the fight-or-flight mechanism and why it should be exploited rather than feared. In unfamiliar situations 'nerves' are normal. Apprehension is normal. You are in a higher gear, that's all, and it feels a bit different. Go with it – *be* exhilarated. Get 'hot under the collar' now and then. Don't let perfectly normal reactions prevent you from doing what you want to do. And for goodness' sake don't let 'stress management' cast a pall of gloom over your life and your emotions, or you really *could* die – of boredom.

Because nervousness is normal, it happens to everybody. Most of us try to conceal it. I've met famous actors and sportsmen who were privately flustered, even terrified, by certain situations, but who because of their jobs had concealment down to a fine art. They *appeared* supremely confident. Some actually overcompensated, so anyone who didn't know them thought they must be conceited.

Of course you don't *have* to conceal your nervousness at all. Simply saying 'I'm very nervous' will disarm most people. They will usually give you the benefit of the doubt as we all know what it's like to have butterflies holding a regatta in our stomachs. Among humans, it's a given. If you perspire a lot, wash well, use anti-bacterial wipes and a good deodorant. If you need to go to the loo, say so. Nobody will think any less of you, unless they themselves have a social handicap that makes them judge other people for peculiar reasons. *You* are in the majority here. Nervous behaviour is what we do when situations matter to us. Who can wonder at that?

BEING 'SHY'

If you are socially inexperienced, of course you are likely to be shy and nervous when you first make contact with other people. Most of us find walking into a roomful of strangers challenging. We do it, though, because we are naturally prone to kinship and would like to find friends and loved ones that we can confide in. So most of us just steel ourselves, walk bravely into the room and start talking – codswallop, probably, until we get into our stride. We become less nervous the more we engage with others, because if you repeatedly face the same situation your level of arousal goes down naturally – without the need for tranquillisers.

Chat rooms

If you needed any proof that other people are shy, just look at the proliferation of Internet chat rooms. Here we have hundreds of thousands of people sidestepping the nervous challenge of walking into a roomful of strangers. If you use chat rooms, you are hoping to 'get to know' people beforehand, so that when you actually meet them, it's a done deal. Except that of course you may be completely deceived by an on-line persona and meet somebody entirely different from the person you imagined. This is because shy people can often fictionalise themselves, and present a front that is as fine a piece of acting as anything seen in a movie.

GO UP AND TALK

Let's suppose then that you are shy, and that you would like to be able to talk to people you don't know, and not wear a mask, and not have to pretend to be someone you are not. Easy – you just go right up and talk to them. So then we hear *another* set of excuses:

- I'm not very good at talking to people.

- I'm not a natural conversationalist.

- I don't have the gift of the gab.

- I'd be no good at selling as I could never persuade.

- Don't ask me to network. I couldn't do it.

- I clam up at interviews.

- I'm rubbish at chatting up the opposite sex.

These are some of the comments I heard over the years from candidates doing our Restart classes. I'll tell you what I told them. You can be good at all of those things.

There's a very simple technique you can learn that will enable you to charm people, chat them up, be good at interviews, network, get the job offers – whatever you like. Plus everybody will think you are totally fab. You just need to understand something that director Keith Johnstone told his nervous actors.

Dialogue happens like this:

1 *A: offers.*

2 *B: accepts.*

3 *Then they continue.*

I don't mean an offer like 'Do you want to buy a washing machine?' I mean **A** might say something like: 'It's a nice day.' **B** *accepts* by saying: 'Yes, it is at the moment, but I think it may rain later.' **A** then *accepts* **B**'s comment and *offers* a new thought: 'I think you're right, but it should be OK for the cricket match.' **B** might *accept* this by asking: 'Oh, do you play cricket?' and **A** might *accept* by replying: 'Yes, but my son won't try it,' and so on. Agreeing to catch the ball somebody is throwing signals that you are willing to play. You throw it back. Game on. Or you can think of it like this: each comment that comes out of the mouths of **A** and **B** is like water flowing from a tap. If **B** turns off the tap, they cannot continue:

> **A**: It's a nice day.
> **B**: No, it isn't.

Or:

> **A**: How are you?
> **B**: Don't ask.

Or:

> **A**: I hear you were in a fight down the Job Centre.
> **B**: Oh, it wasn't anything.

This is 'blocking'. The person answering is shutting down the conversation so that it has nowhere to go, like a train hitting the buffers. In theatre work, scenes spontaneously generate if both actors accept and then offer a new thought. Good improvisers accept 'offers' even if they are very weird, like *Why are you wearing that bloody uniform again, Doris?* The accepting improviser, immediately agreeing to go along with the idea, might reply: *Oh, don't you think it makes my bum look smaller, darling?* As Keith Johnstone says, acceptors seem telepathic and supernatural whereas *bad* improvisers block and suppress the action. They are signalling: 'No, I'm not interested, I won't play, I won't go along with you – I'm leaving you swinging in the wind.'

Good conversationalists – the ones who accept offers and keep the ball in play – appear confident, friendly and successful. They are willing to go on an adventure, even though they don't know where the conversation might lead. Because they are open to offers, they seem interested in the other person, and that in turn endears them because we all like a good listener.

The golden rules of good conversation

1 *Don't agonise over what to say. Just jump in.*
2 *Accept by going along with the other person's idea and then add a new thought. 'Accept' doesn't have to mean 'agree with'. It means be interested, be curious, be open, find out more.*
3 *Ask questions. This keeps the dialogue open and makes the other person feel appreciated.*
4 *Listen. You might actually learn something.*
5 *Look at the other person rather than at your feet or at the cat, or they may think you don't like them.*
6 *Be willing to be nervous. Otherwise you'll never do anything!*
7 *Try saying 'yes' instead of 'no' all the time. Get out of inner jail!*

DOORMATS AND DIVAS

Another reason why those in despair feel that they are not socially successful is this. Whenever they try to engage with other people, somebody ends up *feeling bad*. They either get hurt and embarrassed themselves, or the person they are dealing with gets hurt and embarrassed. Depressed people tend to lack assertiveness. They behave submissively, in which case they get treated as doormats, or they behave aggressively, which means that most of their interactions are doomed to end in flare-ups and resentment.

Doormats have an additional problem that we noticed a lot in our training classes. If they behave submissively – and so get treated with disrespect – for long enough, they may eventually throw a temper tantrum that is completely out of proportion to the situation at hand, and these confrontations often end in abuse or violence. Yet, oddly, doormats and divas may be completely unaware of their own patterns of behaviour. Are *you* a doormat or a diva? See if you recognise yourself in the boxes below.

Doormat behaviour

- *Failing to stand up for yourself or doing so submissively and passively.*

- *Saying what you want or believe in a negative, self-effacing or self-critical way.*

- *Assuming the other person's wants and beliefs matter more than yours.*

- *Assuming they have rights but that you don't.*

- *Assuming that placating others is more important than you are.*

Doormat behaviour achieves recurring defeats.

Diva behaviour

● *Behaving aggressively.*

● *Standing up for yourself without regard to the feelings or wishes of others.*

● *Expressing your desires, rights and opinions while disregarding those of the person you are dealing with.*

● *Assuming that your needs are more important than those of other people.*

● *Assuming that you have rights but that they don't.*

Aggression achieves wins but at the cost of being resented and disliked.

The assertive way is the balanced way. It is the behaviour of mature adults who have learned by experience that fairness usually works and wins friends.

Assertive behaviour

● *Standing up for yourself without apology but without disrespecting or disregarding another person either.*

● *Saying what you want or believe in a straightforward and courteous way.*

● *Recognising your feelings and requirements as well as those of other people.*

● *Understanding that everybody has rights. They do and so do you.*

Assertiveness achieves a win–win outcome in which both parties feel respected.

By mastering this even-handed approach to social situations, you will come away feeling more confident, less resentful, less downtrodden and less red-faced. You will have earned respect and paid it to other people. You won't hurt them and they won't hurt you. Now you can practise this wonderful skill with a friend! Here are some amusing and entertaining exercises to help you.

ASSERTIVENESS EXERCISES

You don't have to do all of these exercises: choose the ones that appeal to you. Ask your friend to take the role of **A**. A can say whatever he or she likes. You should be **B**. Remember – do *not* be rude or aggressive towards them, no matter what they say, but don't be passive either. PRACTISE BEING ASSERTIVE!

Exercise 1

A: You are a very posh waiter in a very exclusive restaurant. You are not used to being questioned by customers about the food.

B: You've just been served a piece of rare chicken.

Exercise 2

A: You are a political activist and you have just walked up the garden path of B. It is crucial to get votes in this area.

B: You are in the middle of something.

Exercise 3

A: You are an elderly dear one who has been placed in residential care. Your relative has come to visit – in fact he or she comes every day, but you don't remember it. So far as you're concerned they haven't been for six months.

B: You are the lucky relative of the dear one.

Exercise 4

A: Your company manufactures calendars. You are very busy.

B: Your company makes strips of paper to stick over the days of the week so the calendars can be re-used. You are on commission only.

Exercise 5

A: You are an American actor and you feel strongly that you are right for this part.

B: You are a British casting director and you already have a British actor in mind.

Exercise 6

A: You have a fish stall down the market but because of the new fishing quotas you haven't actually got any fish. You've got some decent ham.

B: You want fish.

Exercise 7

A: You are the head teacher.

B: You are the parent of a boy who has smashed up the school premises with a club hammer. He is otherwise a typically loveable teenager. You have been asked to see the head teacher.

Exercise 8

A: You are the owner of a dog who has just peed up against the bumper of a very shiny Rolls-Royce.

B: You are the driver of the Rolls, and it isn't your car.

Exercise 9

A: You are a patient at the London Dental Institute. You have had an accident and broken your front teeth. You want implants.

B: You are the dental supervisor and you want to save the NHS money by giving this patient a denture.

As you practise these exercises you will gradually realise the 'balance' required and get a feel for this new method of achieving your objectives without aggression or submission. In fact there *is* no other way to learn this skill other than by practising it.

TAKING THE SOCIAL CHALLENGE

Once you have decided to 'feel the fear and do it anyway', and once you have practised your 'accepting dialogue' skills and your assertiveness skills, *take the social challenge*. Walk into that room, go up and talk to that stranger, approach that person you would like to know, pick up that phone, talk to that influential authority about your idea. Good luck – but you won't need it. It's not luck – it's skill!

USE THIS SPACE TO MAKE A RECORD OF WHAT HAPPENED

The social challenge I chose was:

This is what I did about my nervousness:

The actual exchange went something like this:

What positives did I gain from the exercise?

What will my next social challenge be?

WHAT PANEL MEMBERS THOUGHT

Adrian

'I found this particularly useful – I've always had difficulty in social situations and tend to back off if I meet any resistance. I had assumed that people just didn't want to talk to me. The accepting dialogue was an absolute revelation. I used it at a meeting I was sent to. I tried it with a couple of people and I did notice the difference. I made myself keep the ball in play. It's a boost to your confidence to see the conversation open up before you – "hell, it's me, I'm doing this." I came away thinking, hey, they quite liked me!'

Barbara

'The assertiveness exercises made me laugh because my friends used to say I was a doormat. I see what you mean – it's just putting it into practice. I have lost my temper sometimes because the worm eventually turns, and then there are terrible arguments. I've made up my mind to be more assertive in future because then I won't get to that stage. I think when people say they are shy, they really mean they don't want to get hurt any more. But if you don't try, you don't get. The conversation thing didn't seem to work for me. I couldn't get the hang of it. But then when I was talking to my son I noticed I was doing it automatically. Funnily enough, so was he. It's a kind of rhythm you get into.'

George

'I normally hate doing this kind of thing, but I talked to three people in the village about doing their gardens for them. It's something I've always wanted to do. It doesn't sound much but it was much to me. So with that bit of confidence I went to see the guy who runs the big nursery near here and said I was starting up as a self-employed gardener. I could see he was busy but I kind of wouldn't take no for an answer. He gave me some really practical advice, and some paperwork, and a set of figures to aim for in my first year. He was really friendly at the finish. I can't believe I've done this.'

Charlotte

'You have no idea how difficult this was for me, but I rang up somebody from work, right, pretending I needed some information, but I really just wanted to talk to him again as I quite liked him. To say we just got talking is inaccurate. I was in charge of the whole conversation as I was doing the offering and accepting. I felt it was a bit of a cheat but if it works, go with it. When I put the phone down my hands were sweating as if I'd been in a sauna, but yes. Yes, I would do another challenge – give me another challenge!'

Maggie

'All I ever wanted was to be able to talk to people. These exercises give you hope, and something to fall back on when you're in company. It helps to realise other people may not be confident either. When you aren't dealing with people on a day-to-day basis you think they are all well-rounded individuals and you're the odd one out. You forget they're maybe not, and they get nervous too.'

Five: the mood change challenge

When we are depressed and down, we feel as though our moods are events that happen to us. We simply have to endure them. We might ask the doctor for drugs to make them leave us alone, as though they were bogeymen trying to ruin our lives. If we have a tendency to helplessness, we sit and wait for the prevailing bleak mood to go away. Usually it does *not* go away. It just stays and stays, and we feel worse and worse. If anything bad happens to us while we are in this state, it obliterates what little chinks of light we could see, so that we are left in utter darkness. This is what it is like to be at the bottom of a bottomless pit, sitting there, waiting for things to get better.

You don't have to endure moods at all. To 'suffer' means to allow, as in 'suffer little children to come unto me'. You don't have to 'suffer' from bleak moods. You don't have to 'allow' them to make your life a misery. If you choose to, you can change them. They are not independent events that are happening to your head. When people say, 'cheer up!' they are not trying to annoy or patronise you. They are simply reminding you that you have a choice.

THE 'BEFORE AND AFTER' FACE EXPERIMENT
Try the following experiment. Take your mobile phone camera (or any camera) and by holding it at arm's length take a photo of your face. Don't worry about makeup or smartening up: we're not interested in recording its aesthetic qualities, just *the expression you have written on it*. Now go away and do *one* of the following:

1 *Listen to an upbeat piece of music.*
2 *Find something in a book or on the Internet that amuses you.*
3 *Phone a friend and pay him or her a compliment.*
4 *Go outside and find a tree. Examine it. Put your hands on the bark. If anyone's looking, so much the better. Both hands, please.*

Now, without trying to cheat or distort the findings, take a second picture of your face. Compare the two. If you can't see any difference, show them both to someone you know. The *before* face will be the one you have permitted, and the *after* face will be the one you have chosen to change.

EMOTIONAL VICTIMS AND EMOTIONAL VICTORS

Human emotions are important. Our feelings matter, and your Heartless Bitch is as fierce an opponent of 'stress management' and artificial calm-downs as you are likely to find. But there is a world of difference between sedating emotional arousal on the one hand and enduring long periods of morbid gloom through sheer passivity on the other. This is being an emotional *victim*. Nor is the answer to shove powerful chemicals in your face that interfere with your brain. This is simply more of the same passive style of behaviour. Instead of submitting to the reigning mood, you are submitting to the reigning drug company. If you are currently taking antidepressants, ask your doctor to supervise a recovery programme that will let you stand on your own two feet.

Deliberately altering your prevailing low mood by natural means may strike you as odd, pointless or even vaguely immoral. It may seem in some way 'false'. But it is really none of these. You have a right to change your moods if you don't like them – not as a favour to other people, but as a favour to yourself. Once you have learned to 'kick' morbid moods without using drugs, real empowerment and self-determination become a distinct possibility.

We all admire emotional victors – the ones who, come what may, always seem buoyant and bright. Yet these people are not really any different from you. They have simply chosen *not* to be the victim of their moods. They may have serious problems and they may have to ramp up their courage every day to appear as positive as they do. But they've discovered a few simple psychological laws:

- That if you put a brave face on things, you begin to feel brave.

- That if you smile, you communicate warmth and kindness and others respond accordingly.

- That if you do things that make you feel positive, grateful and cheerful, your expressions will convey the message to other people that you are a force to be reckoned with and a pleasure to know.

The world reflects back the face you show it every day. It holds up a mirror to your moods, and if you choose to enliven these from inside instead of just submitting to whatever bleak gloom comes along, you will find the world looks different, because you will:

**stop being an emotional victim and
start being an emotional victor**.

So how are you feeling? The following challenge is designed to get you off the despair spot.

ENGAGING WITH THE ARTS

The arts specialise in changing our moods. They are designed to do this, and they have done it for generations. You may think 'I am so depressed that I can't face an intellectual stretch.' But that is precisely what you need to do in order to get better. 'Stuck in the doldrums' means *not moving*. 'Petrified' means *turned to stone*. In order *not* to be stuck in the doldrums or petrified, you need to start moving your mind, and *now*.

Choose for your mood challenge at least one of the three art forms below (all three would of course be better). Once you have chosen, you need to:

- engage with the work of art

- give it the full focus of your attention

- get emotionally involved

- finish it.

A great work of art is a whole, and everything in it is there for a reason. It has a beginning, middle and end, and if you quit before the end, you will not understand how it works or experience the transformation it can give you. Set time aside for the exercise, or it will not work and it will not reward you with its optimum effects.

These are the alternatives:

1 a piece of classical music
2 a great work of fiction
3 a cinematic masterpiece.

CLASSICAL MUSIC

There is growing scientific evidence on the benefits of this kind of music to your brain and well-being.[1] If you are unfamiliar with classical music, please expose your senses to one of the following:

- Beethoven's *Egmont* Overture

- Dukas' *The Sorcerer's Apprentice*

- Wagner's *Tannhäuser* Overture

- Ravel's *Bolero*

- Grieg's *Hall of the Mountain King*

- Rossini's *Thieving Magpie* Overture

- Mozart's *Mass in C Minor*, K427 Kyrie.

Classical music is for anyone, regardless of race, creed, class, education or intelligence. It is composed of sequences of sounds that affect the brain. This is music to *lead* your mood, not *follow* it, and apart from being challenging and complex it has rising tension and a climax that you will be able to hear and feel. To make it easier for you to concentrate, especially if you are unused to the classics, you can 'air' conduct, move to it or dance to it. Or you can have a pen and a piece of paper handy and doodle while you listen, or use several colours and paint what you hear. You may be surprised what you come up with.

GREAT WORKS OF FICTION

If you choose a great work of fiction, you may be interested to learn more about the science on the healing power of books. You can find out on the website of the wonderful Reader Organisation, which organises events and reading groups and publicises the latest research.[2] Studies show that reading can cure depression, loneliness and anxiety. An estimated 50% of libraries across the UK are now operating a bibliotherapy scheme, or can put you in touch with a local club or group that meets up regularly to appreciate cracking reads. But whether you choose to delve into great fiction alone or with other people, good books can move your mind.

If you can't think of a great book to try, choose one of the following 20 titles – with a pin if you have never heard of any of them. I compiled the list by asking researchers and librarians for their recommendations for uplifting books, and by asking people who have experienced depression for books that they themselves found illuminating and life-affirming. The titles chosen aren't saccharine and they may not be funny. But they are powerful, can place you in another world and take you on an emotional journey away from the stillness of despair.

84 Charing Cross Road, Helene Hanff
A Christmas Carol, Charles Dickens
Cold Comfort Farm, Stella Gibbons
Empire of the Sun, J. G. Ballard
Fried Green Tomatoes at the Whistle Stop Cafe, Fannie Flagg

Good Grief, Lolly Winston

Jonathan Livingston Seagull, Richard Bach

Like Water for Chocolate, Laura Esquivel

Pride and Prejudice, Jane Austen

Puckoon, Spike Milligan

The Color Purple, Alice Walker

The Darling Buds of May, H. E. Bates

The History of Mr Polly, H. G. Wells

The Life and Loves of a She Devil, Fay Weldon

The River Why, David James Duncan

The Road Home, Rose Tremain

The Secret Magdalene, Ki Longfellow

Walden, Henry David Thoreau

Water for Elephants, Sarah Gruen

Why the Whales Came, Michael Morpurgo

When you have read your chosen book, consider the psychological adventure that it has taken you on and answer the following questions.

Book questionnaire

 1 *Did you feel a kinship with the leading character(s)?*

 2 *What effect did this have on your emotional involvement?*

 3 *Did the character(s) change or develop as a result of what happens?*

 4 *How did the writer manage to involve your feelings?*

 5 *Did you want to know what happened before you reached the ending?*

 6 *Did the ordeals of the people in the story affect you?*

 7 *What did they learn? What did you learn?*

 8 *What was the climax of the story?*

 9 *Did the ending leave you feeling satisfied, or would you have done it differently?*

10 *Suggest how the book might have been different if you had written it.*

11 *Would it have made any difference if the character(s) had given up?*

12 *Did the book move you off the despair spot?*

CLASSICS OF THE CINEMA

If you choose a cinematic masterpiece and don't have a film in mind, you can watch one of the following *that you have not already seen*. They are not all to everyone's taste, because we are all different and we could all argue for months about which movies you should watch. But each of these is challenging, each will make you think and each will make you feel.

- *Gladiator* – the story of an enslaved Roman general who defies an empire, starring Russell Crowe and Joaquin Phoenix, directed by Ridley Scott.

- *Gaslight* – the story of a woman driven to doubt her own sanity by her evil husband, starring Ingrid Bergman and James Mason, directed by George Cukor.

- *Amadeus* – musical genius Mozart is 'murdered' by his rival Salieri, starring F. Murray Abraham and Tom Hulce, directed by Milos Forman.

- *The Shootist* – the redemption of a dying gunslinger starring John Wayne and Lauren Bacall, directed by Don Siegel.

- *Lawrence of Arabia* – the epic tragic tale of T. E. Lawrence, starring Peter O'Toole, directed by David Lean.

- *Brief Encounter* – the story of two happily married people swept away by unfamiliar passion, starring Celia Johnson and Trevor Howard, directed by David Lean.

- *Midnight Cowboy* – the story of a young Texan trying to set up as a stud, starring John Voight and Dustin Hoffman, directed by John Schlesinger.

- *Rainman* – a heartless young man is taken on a journey of discovery by his autistic brother, starring Dustin Hoffman and Tom Cruise, directed by Barry Levinson.

- *Babe* – the story of a pig who thinks he's a sheepdog, starring James Cromwell, directed by Chris Noonan.

Movie questionnaire

1 *Did you feel a kinship with the leading character(s)?*
2 *What effect did this have on your emotional involvement and why?*
3 *Did the character(s) change or develop as a result of what happens?*
4 *Did the music make any difference to your involvement?*
5 *How did the actors and the director manage to reach your feelings?*
6 *As you watched, did you 'want to know what happens in the end'?*
7 *Did the ordeals of those in the story remind you of your life?*
8 *What did they learn? What did you learn?*
9 *What was the climax of the movie?*
10 *Were you satisfied with the plot and the ending?*
11 *How did the movie leave you feeling, and why?*
12 *Did it move you off the despair spot?*

WHAT PANEL MEMBERS THOUGHT

George

'I chose the movie challenge and saw *Amadeus*. I'm not into classical music at all so I wasn't sure what to expect. It knocked me out – the music, the acting, the ending. I wouldn't say the ending was uplifting exactly: it made you angry if anything because it was so shocking. But I forgot all about my own problems and maybe that was the object of the exercise.'

Maggie

'This was magical. I enjoyed my book, *Cold Comfort Farm*, and I enjoyed my piece of music, which was the Mozart *Mass*. Thank you. Yes, we *can* change our moods. The problem is persuading ourselves to actually do it. Depressives tend to, as you say, sit and sit. We need to sit and *enjoy*.'

Barbara

'I didn't want to do any of this. But the fact that you have a choice was the thing that made me think. I've never listened to classical music and I'd never read any of the books on the list. I chose Michael Morpurgo's *Why the Whales Came* and I *really* enjoyed it. It reminded me of my own childhood and how I used to be before I was like this. Yes, I should read more – you make out you don't have the time, but you should make time for yourself. Our local library has a book group now as well so there's no excuse. I also watched *Babe* just because my son liked it. A wonderful film. It cheers you up – my eyes were watering.'

Adrian

'This was the best challenge for me because I liked all the subject areas. The book I chose, *Walden*, was difficult to get hold of, but I eventually got a second-hand copy from Amazon for a couple of quid. This is a genuine transformation book. I think Thoreau cheated because he really lived by the pond for two years rather than one and took his washing home to his mother, but this is a book that stays with you. It makes you look at everything more carefully – even mosquitoes. I'm sure Thoreau knew what it's like to suffer from depression and I respect the way he made himself "go beyond". Yes, it makes sense for us to do these arts challenges and I think anyone who says he is depressed but won't try them is missing out.'

Katey

'Well, this was different, right! On the music front I like modern not classical, so I asked which ones were short. I listened to *Hall of the Mountain King*. It gets louder and louder and you can imagine the old goblins and trolls jumping about. Did it make me feel different? A bit, I suppose. Fair enough, it's only short. The movies seemed to be mostly for men, so I had to pick a black and white, *Gaslight*. I could relate to that though, the way James Mason manipulates his wife by playing mental tricks on her, pretending she's lost his mother's jewellery when he's hidden it. Wicked bastard. Yes, people do that. I've seen it. They better not do it to me.'

Charlotte

'I absolutely loved *Gladiator*. I cheated because I had seen it before, but when you watch it you want to get out of your seat and cheer. Yes, it moves you off the spot. How could anyone watch it and not feel that? Plus Russell Crowe – can't be bad.'

Philip

'I love movies but as I was asked to pick one I'd never seen, I tried *Rainman*. When I'd watched it I rang my own brother up. That's it. You put me bang to rights. How? Well, I don't talk to him and I talked to him.'

NOTES

1. For a brief summary see my book *The Truth About Stress*. Grove Atlantic, pp. 374–7.

2. http://events.thereader.org.uk/get-into-reading-the-reading-cure.html

Six: The nature challenge

Whatever the depth of your despair, Nature can reach you and Nature can rescue you. Even if you normally spend your days in the city and only ever see smoking traffic, brick walls and factory forecourts, your brain will be startled into life by close contact with the green and pleasant land. In fact, if you do spend your days like that, your mind has probably been impaired by such unnatural deprivation and you need to get on with this right away.

The following challenge is designed to get you back into normal communion with Nature. You can do this in two ways: first, by going out into the countryside – or parkland or woods or along a beach; and second, by 'bringing Nature home' – by gardening. Try both, but you must try at least one.

BIG OPEN SPACES

If you don't normally wander in forests and fields or by a sea shore, you may find the whole notion rather alien and put up objections as to why you couldn't possibly do it.

- *I can't afford the fare to get there.*

- *Those places are lonely and I might get attacked.*

- *I'm not mobile enough.*

- *I don't have time.*

- *I suffer from allergies, hay fever, etc.*

- *I'm a townie.*

- *I don't have the proper footwear or clothes.*

- *I'm afraid to go far by myself.*

- *I find big open spaces threatening.*

All of these difficulties can be overcome. If you can't afford the fare, save on something else that you would regard as a leisure activity, such as smoking, drinking, gambling, comfort-eating or retail therapy. If you are on a pension, you may be entitled to a bus pass that will take you far and wide. If you are afraid you might get attacked, get a life. You are just as likely to get waylaid in a town. Besides you don't *have* to choose a particularly lonely spot – pick a place where there are plenty of other people enjoying the views. I've been walking in forests and fields by day and night all my life with my dogs and I'm still here (though as one trainee commented: 'Who'd attack her!').

If you're not mobile enough, please follow the advice for the fitness challenge. Where there's a will, there's a way. 'I don't have time' is an apology for an excuse. *Make* time by using the hour grid and seeing where you can save on time-wasting activities. If you suffer from allergies, get some medical advice. Remember that progressive exposure *de*sensitises and overprotection increases abreaction. We are living in an age where a peanut on the floor can now *clear a school*, so great is our terror of exposure. Unnatural and increasing avoidance of stimuli leads to health dysfunction. In other words, get tough by building up your resistance, and you can start by going out in the fresh air.

'I'm a townie' is the sort of thing one generally hears from people who like to stay out all night pubbing and clubbing and who therefore don't have the energy to get up in the morning. There's no such thing as 'the metropolitan personality'. Anyone can be renewed and refreshed by the countryside, rivers, lakes and sea shores. Anyone can buy a pair of wellingtons or walking shoes and a good warm jacket from a charity shop. You are going where Nature intended, not on a catwalk.

'BARRIER BELIEFS'

The last two objections – 'I'm afraid to go far by myself' and 'I find big open spaces threatening' – are what are known in the life skills professions as 'barrier beliefs'. These are beliefs that prevent us from doing what we would like to do because we will not *test* them and we will not *contest* them. Beliefs like this are tyrants that can rule our lives. The way to overcome them is to:

1 *question them to see if they are true;*
2 *get advice on how to challenge them; and*
3 *challenge them.*

Barrier beliefs are not set in stone. People change their beliefs all the time, sometimes slowly, sometimes dramatically (for example by being converted). A lot of beliefs are out of date and based on what happened to us a long time ago. You are more experienced now, so test old beliefs against your new knowledge. Discuss them with people you trust. Challenging a barrier belief is not as hard as you may think. You are free to act as if you held a different belief. So that might make you nervous – so what?

Brain fishing

Our brains are constantly filtering incoming data – otherwise our heads would be a complete jumble. The brain does this using something called the ascending reticular formation ('reticular' means like a net). The brain net is set to catch particular fish, and it fishes according to the instructions we have given it.

For example, if you tell it to look out for bits of information that confirm your belief that you are fat, it will pick up and capture any chance remark to do with weight, chubbiness, looking cuddly, etc. that seems to confirm the belief held. It lets through the net what doesn't conform to that belief. Yet there are thousands of other bits of data coming in that might disprove that belief altogether. These go through the net and are not retained. The brain is a servo-mechanism. It is doing exactly what you have asked it to do.

We are all 'fishing' all the time, according to our beliefs. So if you reset your net it will soon be looking for positives instead of negatives. And if you hold barrier beliefs that it is fearful to go far by yourself or that big open spaces are threatening, it's time to give your brain net some new fishing quotas!

RECORD YOUR EXPERIENCE

Once you get out into those big open spaces, just passively *being there* may do you the world of good. People who have endured imprisonment and overwhelming pain can find restorative powers in Nature. In fact they can often appreciate more vividly than anyone else the stunning beauty of Nature's simplest sights – the greenness of young stinging nettles, the gloss on the neck of a mallard duck. But if your senses have been dulled by the daily grind, you can certainly heighten your observational powers and become more intimate with Nature by *interacting* with it. One way to do this is by recording the experience, for example by:

- photographing

- sketching

- painting

- tape-recording

- writing.

The great Romantic poets like Samuel Taylor Coleridge and William Wordsworth, whose work celebrated the wonders of wild Nature as none of their predecessors had ever done, recorded their walks and excursions in detail. They invented a new concept – 'interpenetration' – to describe the way in which a person's moods and feelings may be reflected and changed by observing the natural world.

When we closely observe Nature, our perception is altered and we feel ourselves to be part of that natural environment. In Coleridge's famous poem 'This Lime-tree Bower My Prison', for example, the poet's London friends have come to visit. They had all planned to walk in the beautiful Somerset countryside and take in Coleridge's favourite haunts, except that his wife has accidentally spilt boiling milk over his foot and he is lame. So the party goes off without him, and Coleridge sits among the lime trees in a friend's garden feeling very sad and sorry for himself (he was very susceptible to despair as one of the side-effects of taking opium, the 'stress management' of his day). The poem describes the process of Nature healing mood and mind, which is exactly what Nature can do for you too. It ends with:

> ... No plot so narrow, be but Nature there,
> No waste so vacant, but may well employ
> Each faculty of sense, and keep the heart
> Awake to Love and Beauty ...

GETTING INVOLVED WITH NATURE

Here are eight simple ways of 'getting involved with Nature' when you pay it a visit to make your recording:

- **Cloud-spotting**. Observing cloud formations is both rewarding and fascinating. Sunrises and sunsets can be breathtaking. There is even a convenient pocket-sized book to help you with this hobby[1] in which you collect cloud formations and score points, according to how unusual they are. The Cloud Appreciation Society has a website: www.cloudappreciationsociety.org. Or try **stargazing** ...

- **Wildflower and grass count**. Count the number of different wild flowers you can see in the space of, say, a 20-minute walk. Please don't pick them or dig them up as this is illegal and unfair to others. Or you can count the myriad different types of grass – some are extremely beautiful. It's easy to lose track of time and self doing this.

- **Birdwatching**. Or 'twitching' as it is known among aficionados. A lightweight pair of binoculars will enhance your pleasure. You can get help with what you see from the RSPB on www.rspb.org.uk/birdwatch and identify individual birdsongs.

- **Wildlife discovery**. Find a comfortable quiet spot, keep silent and your green surroundings will soon spring to life. If you prefer to be more active, learn to identify the footprints and tracks of wild animals like badgers, deer and foxes and follow their trails.

- **Tree bark 'sculptures'**. You can train yourself to be more imaginatively observant by looking for sculptured shapes and 'faces' in tree bark (gnarled old oaks and beech trees are best). If you record them you can get some amusing and amazing results to show friends.

- **Fungus spotting**. The best time for this is obviously autumn. Count and record the many different types of exotic and interesting fungi and learn about their properties. Be careful as some are extremely poisonous, but their beauty and variety of structure will intrigue you.

- **Insect study**. If you turn over a rotten log in a field, a little world reveals itself of scurrying and scanty beasties that may be new to you. One of the most secretive things I ever saw in our nature reserve was the body of a tiny dead shrew, apparently moving smoothly along the ground by itself. Beneath it were three sexton beetles, bright yellow and black, taking the body away for burial. Such wonders abound. You just have to go out and look for them.

- **Beachcombing**. Find a beach, find the tide-line, get there before anybody else and search for mysterious and wonderful objects. Then you could turn them into something artistic for your creative challenge.

GARDENING

How can gardening possibly help someone in despair?

> *To survive in prison, one must develop ways to take satisfaction in one's daily life*
> *... To plant a seed, to watch it grow, tend to it and then harvest it, offered a*
> *simple but enduring satisfaction. The sense of being the custodian of this small*
> *patch of earth offered a taste of freedom ...*

This is Nelson Mandela talking about how he kept sane during his long years of imprisonment. It comes from a very uplifting book about torture victims who have been helped to rebuild their shattered lives by planting, tilling, hoeing and growing, called *The Healing Fields*.[2] For these desolate people, working with Nature enabled them to communicate what they felt. It gradually brought them back from their lonely inner darkness into daylight.

Grow something!

Your gardening challenge is simply to *grow* something of your very own. Bring Nature home to you by going along to your local nursery and buying seeds (very cheap) or bulbs, a bag of compost and a tub or pot to put them in. Ask for advice on what you need and read the instructions on the packaging. With a little initiative and planning you can grow pleasures for your eyes, scents for your nose and delicious vegetables for your dinner.

If you are lucky enough to have a garden, choose a particular patch that you can dig over and make it your 'Garden of Contentment' to attract birds, butterflies and bees. Sketch out a plan first, and decide on the colours, heights and foliage you will need. Then begin preparing the soil for your planting. Put your hands in it – that is the good earth! You don't need a big space for your purposes: tubs and climbing plants work extremely well in a tiny walled town garden. As your Garden of Contentment becomes established you can make it more exotic by including a small inexpensive water feature.

If you have no garden, choose window displays or indoor plants, or check out local allotment spaces. The important thing is that you should grow and tend something you plant and see it come to fruition. As Nelson Mandela says, it will give you enduring satisfaction and a taste of freedom.

WHAT PANEL MEMBERS THOUGHT

Maggie

'I can't praise gardening highly enough. No matter what I've been through the previous night, a morning in my little garden and a cup of coffee will bring me back to life. Nature offers you everything: beauty, originality, complexity, simplicity. I'm not terribly mobile these days but I do go over my neighbour's garden which looks out onto open fields, and I sit watching the deer and the foxes. It makes life worthwhile again. How can anyone *not* love Nature? What's not to love?'

Terry

'I wish I'd done gardening when I was younger but I thought it was for old farts. A lot of old blokes round here have an allotment strip and they all seemed fitter than me, so I've never done anything like this but I asked their advice and I grew some tomatoes in a grow-bag just inside my porch. It was a nuisance at first with the mess and the watering etc., but I ate them and wow! They were much better than what you get in the supermarket, and the point was, *I bloody grew them*! It does give you a sense of satisfaction and you don't have to know a lot to get started. Anybody can do it. Anybody can apply for an allotment strip. Why not, if it saves you money?'

Susanna

'I do sometimes have a feeling of panic when I'm alone out in the open but I find if I have a friend with me I can manage it. We chose "looking for sunsets" as my project, sitting over the sports field. Often you don't get anything because of the cloud so you have to be patient. But then one evening you'll get a really glorious one. The best was when I was there on my own and it was a complete fluke as I was just testing myself to see if I could do it. I started taking photos on my mobile. You get lovely golds and peach colours, not just red, and they are never two the same. I don't know what it is about the horizon, but hope does come from there.'

Charlotte

'What does Nature mean to me? Walking across the grass with no shoes on. Everyone should try it. It's the only time I don't think about what I look like. Yes, I see the point. I think if I did it more often I might not worry so much about stupid things.'

Philip

'For my challenge I got my bike out and cycled down to Heybridge Basin. I didn't think I'd be in any shape after not much sleep but I took it easy and it wasn't that bad. I sat on a newspaper looking out at the sea, smoking I'm afraid, but I did have a sandwich! When I got home I'd caught the sun. That's a funny phrase, if you think about it. You catch it and then you bring it indoors. Yes, I felt better. You always do if you get out.'

Vaz

'I'm not doing any of that. I'm a townie.'

NOTES

1. Gavin Pretor-Pinney, *The Cloud Collector's Handbook*. Sceptre, 2009.

2. Sonja Linden and Jenny Grut, *The Healing Fields*. Frances Lincoln in association with the Medical Foundation for the Care of Victims of Torture.

Seven: the performance challenge

If you have read the first section of the book and done the first six challenges you will by now be familiar with the idea of 'facing the monster' – turning towards a task that may make you apprehensive or afraid and preparing to deal with it.

NERVES ARE GOOD, BORING IS BAD

You will be familiar with what is popularly known as the 'adrenalin rush' when you have decided to go ahead. You will know that this is not a sign of incipient madness or a kind of disease called 'stress' or anything else abnormal – because everyone experiences it. You will have discovered that your heightened state of nervousness is part of the complex system of preparation to raise your game in the face of a challenge or threat. You will *also* have learned that the more you face a particular challenge, the less aroused you will feel, until you are finally so relaxed about it you may look round for something else that is 'more of a challenge'.

So here now is an exciting thing for you to do, one that will put the colour in your cheeks and make you feel life is for living. If you are feeling depressed before you start, the exhilaration of this challenge will flush out your system and recharge your batteries. You may even experience the spark from heaven that goes by the name of inspiration.

ON THEIR HIND LEGS

The performance challenge can cause a lot of apprehension, especially for those who have never tried it before. This is precisely why I want you to do it. My trainees were required to get up on their hind legs in front of our (sometimes very large) classes and give presentations and perform sketches. Many of them regarded it with dread. We would have everything from murmurings of inadequacy to angry outbursts and outright refusals to cooperate (I had papers and the odd chair thrown etc.). I would not brook 'no' for an answer because I knew that unemployed people may be required by potential employers to give presentations, give an account of themselves, perform to order. If they could not do this, they would be unlikely to impress in a highly competitive market.

Despite their initial objections each and every person on the course had to do his or her performance challenge. I would involve the rest of the class in cheering, calling for them to get on with it etc., and in the end the reluctant performer would stumble or crawl to the front and give anything from a reasonable version of what they had in mind, but with a few mistakes which did not matter in the context of their wonderful courage, to the most astonishing *tour de force* that came from they knew not where.

When they sat down I would ask them how they felt. Typically their faces would be flushed, and they would snigger or shrug and say something inconsequential like 'Oh, it wasn't so bad' or 'I could have done it better'. But I knew by their demeanour that they had made an inner discovery, one that they could not possibly have made in any other way than by doing the performance challenge.

Your challenge will be to:

- **give a talk on a subject of your choice**

- **perform a sketch (alone or with other people)**

- **give a musical performance**

- **present and demonstrate a skill of your choice**

- **perform in a play.**

Whatever you choose will require some work and commitment from you. Ideally an element of theatre should be introduced.

You may of course prefer something not on the list, and that's fine so long as it involves genuinely *performing*. For your audience you may choose either to invite a group of friends to sit and watch or request to perform at a venue in front of strangers – on a stage, in a hall, theatre, club, pub, etc. One very rewarding venue is to perform for people in a retirement home. If you ring up and say you would like to entertain the residents, you will be offering a lifeline to folk who are frequently bored out of their skulls and who would be very appreciative of even the most modest skills. You can even busk in the street if you like, though this generally requires a licence. What you achieve will be up to you, but the exercise will dispel the inner darkness of 'never daring to do anything'. If you have a couple of friends willing to help you, you might try something that my trainees found huge fun and that often brought the house down. It was this:

> **Chat show sketch**
> *You are a chat show host. You have two or three 'guests'. Your job is to think what you will ask them and how you will link them (they don't have to be living people). You then set up your furniture, introduce yourself and your star 'guests' to the audience and then make it up as you go along. Your 'guests' don't have to know anything about their subject areas at all. They can just busk it as well. The more absurd, the better the audience seem to like it.*

If you choose to give a presentation, I shall explain how to do this below. If you would like to perform a sketch or a play, you can either select something already written or – far more exciting – write the thing yourself. Or your choice might be to perform some music, perhaps by singing in a competition or in a choir, or as part of a karaoke evening. You might prefer playing a musical instrument or performing a dance. If you choose 'demonstrate a skill', this will allow you to do anything from playing the spoons to showing how to grow potatoes. Among our unemployed trainees there emerged extraordinary hidden talents from *trompe l'oeil* (optical illusion paintings) to walking across the floor on all fours facing the ceiling – which fetched huge applause. The important thing is to get out there and do it.

PRESENTATION SKILLS

Presenting a talk to a paying audience carries the responsibility of delivering value for money. On the other hand, you have the advantage of an audience who will shut up and listen to you – at least initially. But giving a talk to people who may not have chosen to hear you, who may not believe you or who may not share your enthusiasm is another matter. It's tough. So why bother? Because if you can do this:

- interviews and meetings hold no fears for you

- you can put together a proposal, a synopsis, a case

- you can sell (package) an idea

- you can persuade

- you can think in a crisis

- you can jump in when others hold back

- you can overcome negativity and cynicism

- you can communicate enthusiasm.

TWO KINDS OF PRESENTATION

There are two basic kinds of talk or presentation: those where you prepare and those where you extemporise. For the second you need to use improvisation skills and fly by the seat of your pants. *Either* may make you nervous. So which is better – to prepare carefully beforehand so that you leave nothing to chance, or to jump in without any idea how you will do it and just improvise?

STAGE FRIGHT

I once worked with a doctor who in the course of his work was required to give presentations at conferences. He didn't like doing them because they made him apprehensive, so he tried an experiment on himself. He videoed his performance when he had taken tranquillisers, and he videoed his performance when he had not. To his surprise, he decided the second was better. The sedated performance was smooth but it was somehow lifeless. It was predictable, and the audience responded politely and respectfully.

In the second performance (without the drugs) his hands shook slightly and he made a couple of trivial mistakes. But he was more alive, more responsive to the audience and therefore able to adapt his material. He was also more appreciated. The audience warmed to him as someone who was speaking to them personally. They wanted to 'hear the next bit' because they weren't sure what he would say. Because nothing was pat, the timing and the laughs were genuine. There was a human being on the stage instead of an automaton, so he found himself working in an atmosphere of fascination and support. This doctor never took tranquillisers for his presentations any more.

ELEVEN TIPS FOR PREPARING TALKS

If you have the time and the inclination to organise your talk beforehand, there are certain generally recognised rules for success:

1 **Define the purpose of your talk**. What's your point?

2 **Know your audience**. Who are the people who will be listening? Define your objective – sell, convince, convert, entertain, motivate, shock, inspire or make them laugh?

3 **Know the setting**. Familiarise yourself with the room or stage and the technology you may be using (e.g. PowerPoint, overhead projection).

4   **Give it a structure**. Audiences learn best from a series of chunks depending on length – about six is the optimum. So be selective about your chunks. If possible, keep a theme running through and branch off. The conventional wisdom is to begin with an introduction that *includes your conclusion*.

5   **Use real examples, analogies or visual aids to make it memorable**. Keep the audience interested by using something dramatic or personal such as:
a reference to the occasion
a startling statement
an anecdote.

6   **Have a heart to your talk**. This contains all the important information and ideas – not just a list. Use evidence to substantiate your comments.

7   **Make your conclusion**. Sum up your main point for easy memorising. Signal the end by saying 'Finally' or 'Before I draw to a close'. Then finish with something punchy.

8   **Get your timing right**. Less is more, and never overrun. Build using seven-minute blocks. You must control time – make sure you can see the clock.

9   **Rehearse but not parrot-fashion**. Use key words and prompt cards. Never, ever just read a speech. Audiences will turn against you and regard you as dull and spineless.

10 **Get personal**. Make eye contact with people in the audience. Give your preparation individual touches that could only come from you. Keep to your own personal style and include things that amuse you.

11 **Finally – love your subject**. Enthusiasm is contagious and people admire speakers with motivation.

FLYING BY THE SEAT OF YOUR PANTS

Of course, you may not want to prepare a set talk like this at all! Having chosen your subject and the general points you wish to convey, you may prefer to make it up as you go along. If that's the case, then you will need to practise – not practise *your talk*, but practise *flying by the seat of your pants*. So here's what to do.

Photocopy the following list of 'problems to be solved' and then cut them into narrow strips, one problem per strip. Roll the strips up tightly so that you can't read them beforehand, and put the little paper pellets in a lid or bag. Now in front of somebody *else*, pick out a 'fortune cookie' at random (you can let them have a turn, too, or they may refuse to cooperate). Finally, without *even giving it a moment's thought* explain how to solve the problem you have just unwrapped. You can't possibly 'do this wrong': chances are you won't know how to solve any of these problems *at all*. So you'll just have to make something up on the spot. Good luck – you won't need it.

> **Fortune cookie problems**
>
> 1   *How to be a good Kenneth Williams impersonator*
> 2   *How to tell a small child where it came from*
> 3   *How to sell your new invention of floating soap to a sponsor*
> 4   *How to predict the weather*
> 5   *How to persuade a scientist to believe in horoscopes*
> 6   *How to avoid trouble with a visitor from another planet*
> 7   *How to handle a New Age Traveller parked in your garden*
> 8   *How to make a traffic warden tear up your ticket*
> 9   *How to feed the five thousand*
> 10 *How to have a good time with Robert Mugabe*
> 11 *How to cheer up somebody whose horse came in last*
> 12 *How to fish for compliments*
> 13 *How to avoid dust mites in your bed*
> 14 *How to look for a silver lining*
> 15 *How to hide a pimple on your nose for a TV interview*
> 16 *How to win sympathy from the Inland Revenue*

17 *How to manage on a desert island with only a lizard for company*

18 *How to dance the polka*

19 *How to dive off the 10-metre board*

20 *How to sell fish fingers to the French*

21 *How to sleep in a haunted house*

22 *How to sell Big Ben to a Texan billionaire*

23 *How to deal with somebody who keeps following you about*

24 *How to ride a motor bike with no hands*

25 *How to persuade the Tate Modern to exhibit your old fridge*

26 *How to teach ski jumping for beginners*

27 *How to shear a sheep*

28 *How to get a bee out of your bonnet*

29 *How to teach a dog to bark up the right tree*

30 *How to help a colour-blind driver at traffic lights*

31 *How to give Henry VIII the slip in Hampton Court Maze*

32 *How to travel light*

33 *How to make a silk purse out of a sow's ear*

34 *How to race pigeons*

35 *How to find the lost city of Atlantis*

36 *How to see round corners*

KEEPING A RECORD

When you have completed your challenge, keep a record here of what happened so that when you do other challenges you can compare methods you used and find out which worked best for you.

MY PERFORMANCE CHALLENGE

The performance I chose was:

My audience was:

My preparations were as follows:

My feelings before the event were:

My feelings after the event were:

This is what I might have done differently:

Congratulations! There was, incidentally, no way *not* to succeed at this. If you plucked up the courage to attempt it, then you have achieved something wonderful and worthwhile that will stand you in good stead for trying other things. The only failure is not to have tried.

WHAT PANEL MEMBERS THOUGHT

Katey

'I knew you'd pick on me for this! OK, I didn't do a gig or anything. It was only a karaoke evening at the pub where I've been before with my mates. But I did sing *two* songs – as I got an encore. The first one I made a couple of mistakes with the lyrics but then I got into my stride and I was like – *look at me, mum!* I haven't done anything like this for ages. I had a strange feeling that I was meant to do it. Not because I'm amazingly talented or anything, but I just felt – this is *what I do*, so bring it on. That's going to sound really big-headed. Can you take that bit out?'

Susanna

'My God, I thought, I've never got up on a stage in my life. So my friend Anna, who is a teaching assistant, and her colleague and some of the kids agreed to be my audience and I did a piece I got from a book by Richard Louv, about a little child playing in bad weather. Except that it gradually got more elaborate in the planning, and in the end I illustrated it with photographs and props, including a costume, a mud pie and a piece of plastic guttering that I poured water down with a jug so I got completely soaked. But when I finished they gave me a huge round of applause. It brought tears to my eyes to think I'd done such a strange rewarding thing. I don't know if I could perform in front of a *real* audience but you never know till you try.'

Adrian

'I did an actual departmental seminar presentation. I do these with dread. But it went extremely well actually. I didn't follow the set rules but I did prepare to some extent beforehand as I get terribly nervous. What surprised me was my ability to think "on the hoof", as it were, as I don't normally leave any breathing space for myself and do wall-to-wall preparation that is ultimately very restricting. I think it would have been far less interesting than the experience I had. I would recommend this for anyone who is depressed – not formal presentation necessarily, but some kind of performance. It makes you think outside the box and gives you a glow of inner satisfaction that you had the guts to get up there and do it.'

George

'Following on from the Restart course my partner and I asked if we could go round to the local care home just before Christmas and we gave a little show, based on Dame Edna and a couple of other bits and pieces. It was absolutely bloody *fantastic*. They made such a fuss of us that we agreed to do it next year as well. I think they got us drunk actually but I took a lot of photos and it was one of those things that you look back on and get a catch in your throat.'

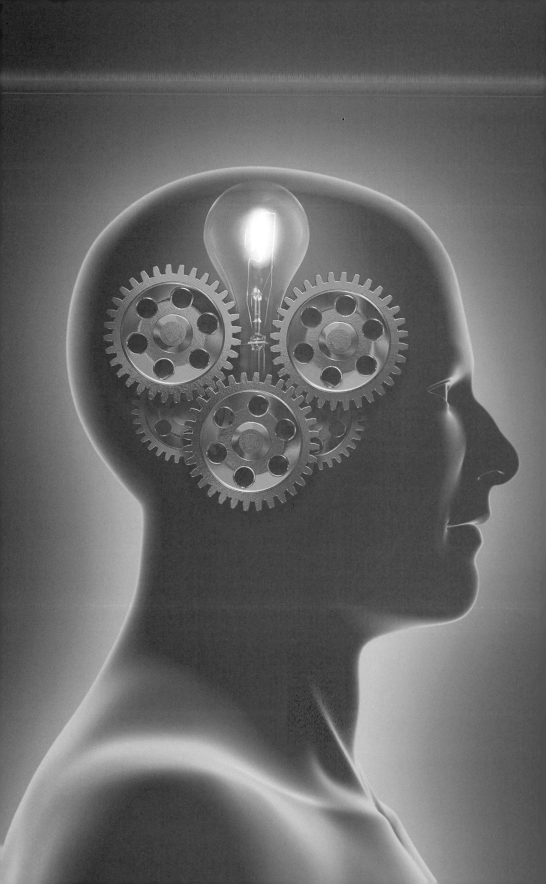

Eight: the creative challenge

Having gone through the earlier challenges, you will have learned something about human psychology that no book can teach you. The word 'peril', and the words 'experience', 'experiment' and 'expert', all derive from the Latin *experiri*, meaning 'to try thoroughly' or 'put to the test'. Negative emotions including fear and tension are part of the rich cerebral process that makes possible our creativity, our peak experiences and our joy. We don't achieve *expertise* in anything unless we are prepared to be put to the test. We don't achieve understanding or mastery of our feelings unless we are willing to *experiment*. We don't *experience* anything either, apart from useless anxiety and despair that haunt our lives.

The Creative Challenge is one of the best and most rewarding challenges of all. It is one that can haul someone out of the well of despair like a cat being winched up in a bucket. If you imagine that you are not creative, you are wrong and we can prove it.

YOU *ARE* CREATIVE!
Let's start with a Brain Quiz.

Question 1
This one is about your brain's storage capacity. How many brain cells do you have?

(a)   30 million
(b)   10 billion
(c)   12

The answer is none of them. You have 100 billion or 10 to the power of 11. And each connects up with 10,000 others, which means multiple quadrillions of connections.

> **Scientist Dr Mark Rosenweig**: Even if your brain were fed ten items of data every second for 100 years, it would still have used less than one tenth of its storage capacity.

Question 2

What does your brain look like inside?

> **Golgi's silver nitrate**
>
> The first person to see individual neurons was the Italian scientist Camillo Golgi. He won the Nobel Prize but it was all an accident. In 1972 he knocked a piece of brain tissue into a solution of silver nitrate and didn't notice his mistake for several weeks.
>
> When he looked at it again and examined slices under a microscope, he saw that some cells had filled up with the nitrate and therefore showed up against the brightly lit background.
>
> A neuron, he was amazed to discover, was a rounded cell body, between one two hundredth and one tenth of a millimetre across, with a number of fine fibres growing out into the surrounding tissue. The longest, and it can grow up to a metre in some types of cell, winding and twining its way through the brain's circuits, is the axon or transmission cable. The others are dendrites or receivers.

Question 3

This one is about the brain's blood supply. Your brain is just over 2% of your body weight. What proportion of your glucose and oxygen does it consume?

(a)   20%

(b)   10%

(c)   1%

The answer is (a), 20% of the glucose and oxygen *needed by your whole body*. You see now why the fight-or-flight response must reorganise your blood supply when you face a challenge or threat, so that your brain can 'charge up' ready for action.

HEMISPHERES

Your brain resembles a very large walnut, with two halves joined together. Scientists have found that the right and left hemispheres broadly specialise in different styles of thinking, like this:

Left brain	Right brain
words (grammar, sentences)	words (poetry, images)
numbers	rhythm
logic	spatial awareness
particulars	gestalt (wholeness)
sequence	imagination
linearity	daydreaming
lists	colour
analysis	dimension

Hemispheres task

You have a reproduction Roman centurion's helmet that you wish to sell. Using only left *brain specialities design an advertisement to be posted on eBay highlighting its selling points.*

Repeat the exercise, this time using only right *brain specialities.*

Which was harder?

IMAGINATION

The 'imagination' refers literally to the right *imaging* hemisphere. Your brain's ability to recall and store images is prodigious and much more accurate than recall of names. If you want to remember a list of items, you can do this by using image mnemonics – by converting each into a picture so that your brain can store it more readily. It is much easier to teach a child to ride a bike or a man to swing a golf club if you *show* them how to do it rather than trying to tell them. To the brain, a picture really is worth a thousand words.

Everyone has an imaging right brain. A lot of people are afraid to use it. If you think you can't draw, for example, take a look at *Drawing on the Right Side of the Brain* by Dr Betty Edwards.[1] This astonishing book is about people who thought they were incapable of sketching – and if you examine their original efforts you would have to concur: no artistic gifts here. Matchstick figures and lollipop trees – just amateur symbols of the real things. But Dr Edwards took these same people and trained them to look at, and into, objects in a calm, focused, meditative state. They were now using not the left brain, with its judgemental and analytical powers, but the imaginative right brain. *Now* they could see their subjects! This different way of *seeing* enabled each 'cannot draw' artist to produce sketches that were graphically so much more accurate and real that they appeared to be by somebody else.

You can use your creative right brain in all sorts of ways. If you like sudokus, for example, the way that you probably work them out now is by using logic and numerical skills. But next time you get stuck, try allowing your eyes to relax and 'take in' the patterns. Pretty soon you will find your gaze drawn to a match for the surrounding numbers or a significant blank square that will provide the missing clue.

You can practise relaxing your gaze with those popular '3D pictures' that you can find in many bookshops. These are collections of coloured patterns that, when gazed at in a certain relaxed way, reveal hidden figures and shapes that seem to stand proud of the page. Some people claim they can never see anything. This is because they are obstinately using their left brains and trying to force their logical intelligence to 'solve' the patterns whereas what they need to do is to relax their eyes and gently *allow* the figures to emerge. A little patience may be needed. If the imaginative right brain has been cowed down by a lot of left brain discipline and activity, it may take a while to venture out and do its stuff.

However left-brain we may have become in this increasingly mechanical society, we all experience imaginative thinking, whether we like it or not – as we are about to drop off to sleep. Between waking and sleeping our brains present us with what are known as *hypnagogic* images – pictures, illogical sequences and memories, sometimes with narrative links but often not, that simply 'pop' unbidden into our minds. If we try to seize them they are gone, like the colours in a dragonfly's wings.

OFF WITH THE FAIRIES

When we are entranced by an activity – whether it be embroidering, making a chair leg or shaping a garden pond – we are 'off with the fairies'. Time and space do not matter. Our problems, our concerns, even ourselves, do not matter. We have entered another dimension – the creative, right-brain, imaginative dimension where anything is possible. This is the dream time of the Australian aboriginal and the cave painter, the artist and the child. These are the lost faculties that Western society has proscribed as time-wasting, illogical, mad and inappropriate. But this is the dimension you can inhabit if you allow yourself to look more gently at the world – and create. People usually start off as creative children and become inhibited adults. They shrink from rejection. Then they get married, mortgaged, bored and buried. Let's wake up now and enjoy being brilliant, as anyone can, while we are alive and still able to do it.

What we produce in our ego-less imaginative state is in a way *separate from us*. It may be inspired. Poet and novelist William Makepiece Thackeray spoke for all writers and artists when he said: 'I have been surprised at the observations made by some of my characters. It seems as if an occult power were moving my pen.'

ORIGINALITY

Consider the following valuation puzzle:

- A great painting may be worth millions.

- A print, though it may look almost exactly the same, might be worth just a few pounds.

- A forgery is worth nothing.

Why? Because as a society we value originality *per se*. Indeed we revere it. We celebrate original writers, poets, painters, actors, sportsmen, fashion designers, dancers, composers, television performers – virtually as demigods. Not all of us can be original – *or can we*? Here is a little test for you. Please answer the questions as honestly as you can.

The shape of things to come

1 *What do other people think you are good at?*
2 *What do you think you are good at?*
3 *What do you do that is different or unique?*
4 *What have you yourself created, made or manufactured?*
5 *What might be considered your hidden talent?*
6 *What inspires you?*
7 *If you were to produce something now that was new and original, what would it be?*
8 *WHY ARE YOU NOT DOING IT?*

THE SCREEN-STARING SOCIETY

We live in a screen-staring society (teenagers are even referred to now as *screen*agers). People stare into screens, shovelling food and drinks in their faces, and then go to bed and dream of what might have been.

Being constantly exposed to other people's creations, we may think all the original things in the world have already been done. You may say: 'I could never produce anything like *that* person.' No, you will only produce anything like *that* person if you set out to imitate him or her. In fact one of the biggest inhibitors to originality is the desire to *be* original.

Just be yourself. Follow your own trail of salt. *Don't try to be original*. In improvisation work it kills the imagination stone dead. You already ARE original. In fact you are unique. You are the only person in the universe who knows everything you know and has felt everything you have felt. All you have to do is step aside and allow your right brain some freedom. Your imagination already *has* all the connections. Edit what it produces once you've got it. Not before.

HOW TO 'STEP ASIDE'?

There are various techniques one can use. Improvisation games work wonderfully – you can use those we tried earlier or make up new ones. Meditation is another: if you simply focus on a candle flame and clear your mind, imaginative ideas will often present themselves. Tennis players who use Tim Gallwey's 'Inner Game' technique focus on the seams of the ball as it turns over in the air, and golfers visualise the ball's trajectory to free up *their* inner game. Some people prefer hypnosis. Sergei Rachmaninov composed his world-famous Second Piano Concerto after sessions with a hypnotist telling him: 'You will compose with great facility'. Self-hypnosis, in which you play back tapes you have recorded yourself, can be useful too. Or you might try this:

Distracting the editor

You are a journalist in a busy newspaper office. You are really very creative, but your editor is the sort of mechanical, judgemental bully that constantly interferes with your writing and puts you off. Have a pen and paper in front of you, or sit at your PC ready to type.

Now distract your inner 'editor' by giving him a task: 'counting down from 100' or 'reciting the alphabet backwards' are the sort of 'clever clever' assignments that will appeal to him and keep him busy for a few minutes. Meanwhile, allow your imagination, during this window of opportunity, to just type or scribble away!

See what you get – and by the way, there is absolutely no point in cheating.

Having used whatever 'freeing-up' method you prefer, take the Creative Challenge!

Make something, write something, compose something, ornament or embellish something (for example by carving or embroidery), paint something, draw something, manufacture something, sculpt something, mould something, build something, model something, choreograph something, paper-fold something, paste something, formulate something, decorate something, sew something, knit something, crochet something, design something, computer generate something, glass-blow something, stone-craft something, script something. Whatever ...

But bring something into being that has never existed before.

Learning to exercise the creative imagination can enable depressed people to re-enter the world of wonder and hope. It is both rewarding and life-affirming. *Go create.*

WHAT PANEL MEMBERS THOUGHT

Charlotte

'I've started a semi-fictional sort of journal. When I was a patient at the big London clinic where I was being treated for body dysmorphia, someone there suggested I keep a diary, but this is different. It's partly about me but partly not. I'm finding it's a useful way of getting my feelings out there without necessarily losing my privacy. Actually there's a lot in it that is pure fantasy and enjoyable to do.'

Philip

'When I did the "count down from 100" exercise, nothing came out. Not a bloody sausage. I tried making a jewellery box using off-cuts but that was rubbish. So I thought, what can I do? Well, I was ringing into the local radio station at about two in the morning talking about some alcoholic in the news when it suddenly came to me. I'll make some beer-mats. I might even sell them. I cannibalised veneers and timber off-cuts, squared them up and bevelled the edges, dyeing them different colours and gluing them together. I was really quite chuffed with them. I've seen other home-crafted ones but mine were just as good, if not better. I have made things before but never while I've been depressed.'

Vaz

'Would "making a baby" count? That's creative, isn't it – the ultimate! Anyone who is a parent knows what "go create" really means. But when I've been totally down, I didn't even want to do that. I'm a bit better now, it has to be said. Oh, and I had a bit of a dance round the bedroom. That gets your blood circulating. OK, I am trying, honest!'

Susanna

'I decorated the little spare room. I'm not that handy but I did it all, floor to ceiling, and wouldn't let anybody help me. I even decorated the lampshade. Then I looked at the clock and it was half past one in the morning! But I love making things. While you're decorating or embroidering or knitting, you're in another world, and you look up and the clock's gone round and you can't say where you've been. It's great when you're feeling down because something else takes over. There can be a war going on outside and you're just there, humming away to yourself, quite contented.'

Barbara

'I made a rabbit for my granddaughter – she's only three but quite intelligent. I cut out all the pieces first from an old fake fur coat I'd never worn, and I had a struggle getting the needle through as the fabric was very thick, but then as you begin to assemble it, it all starts to look like what you imagined you were making. When I showed it to my granddaughter she thought I'd bought it. I said, "No, I made it for you, my darling." I think one ear fell off but I sewed it back on again and she takes it to bed with her.'

Adrian

'I'm madly creative but in bursts. I do scattergun writing – bits of fiction, bits of observation. This was more disciplined. I wrote some material for a trade magazine – I can't be more specific – but they liked it. They said they would quite possibly commission something on a different theme, but what was more important to me was that they said I could write. I know I can, but I usually don't own it. I don't sign it and I don't feel responsible for it. This had my by-line on it. It is a modest breakthrough. At least I'm getting paid.'

NOTE

1. Originally published by HarperCollins in 1993 but there are several revised versions.

Nine: the fear challenge

Let's begin with a puzzle for you to solve.

THE SCARED DOG PUZZLE

I have a retired greyhound who is terrified of bird-scarers – compressed air cylinders emitting loud timed explosions that are intended to frighten birds away from farmers' crops. They are set to go off at intervals of perhaps twenty minutes, and may be positioned near footpaths. Wherever I walk my dog in the countryside where we live, he can hear these explosions, and they can go on for months. What should I do about this problem?

1 Not walk my dog.

2 Walk my dog around the town only.

3 Keep pushing and pulling my dog forward even though he is scared.

4 Sedate my dog.

5 Train my dog to get used to loud noises by playing him recordings.

6 Inure my dog to the bangs by sitting in the car with him nearby.

If you answer (1), under new animal welfare legislation this may constitute cruel or improper treatment and my dog could be taken away. If you think (4), veterinary drugs can be very expensive and may cause side effects. If you answer (3), my dog is very large and therefore difficult to manoeuvre. And if you say (2) I should have to pay for a lot of extra petrol and parking fees in order to give my dog a rather unnatural life. When I sought professional advice from a vet and an animal behaviourist, one said (5) and the other said (6). *Why?*

PHOBIAS GALORE!

If you look on the Internet under 'phobias' you will find a virtual cornucopia of terrors. Here is just a *tiny* selection:

achluophobia	fear of darkness
acousticophobia	fear of noise
acrophobia	fear of heights
agliophobia	fear of pain
agoraphobia	fear of open spaces
aichmophobia	fear of needles
arachnophobia	fear of spiders
astraphobia (brotophobia)	fear of thunder and lightning
ataxophobia	fear of disorder, untidiness
atychiphobia	fear of failure
autophobia	fear of being alone
aviophobia	fear of flying
cenophobia (centophobia)	fear of new things or ideas
claustrophobia	fear of confined spaces
climacophobia	fear of stairs
coulrophobia	fear of clowns
cyberphobia	fear of computers
cynophobia	fear of dogs
decidophobia	fear of making decisions
demophobia	fear of crowds
dentophobia	fear of dentists
didaskaleinophobia	fear of education
erotophobia	fear of sex
gamophobia	fear of marriage
gerontophobia	fear of old age
glossophobia	fear of public speaking
lockiophobia	fear of childbirth
lygophobia	fear of darkness
musophobia (muriphobia)	fear of mice

- necrophobia — fear of death
- nudophobia — fear of nudity
- nyctophobia — fear of night
- ophidrophobia — fear of snakes
- phalacrophobia — fear of baldness
- scolionophobia — fear of education
- spheksophobia — fear of wasps
- tachophobia — fear of speed
- technophobia — fear of technology
- tomophobia — fear of surgery
- xenophobia — fear of foreigners, strangers

Two that I particularly liked were *hexakosioihexekontahexaphobia*, or fear of the number '666', and *anophobia*, which is fear of everything! I have no idea what you might be afraid of. Your particular bogeymen may not be here at all because there are literally *hundreds* more phobias to choose from. But take a look at my short selection for a moment. Examine it, and let your eyes run up and down. I want you to consider a very radical idea about all these phobias – one that may get you to see your own fears in a completely new light.

It is not the *thing* that you are afraid of; it is the *fear*.

It has long been recognised – and not just by psychologists – that fear is self-perpetuating and self-augmenting. Franklin D. Roosevelt warned America in his first inaugural address in 1933: 'There is nothing to fear but fear itself.' Roosevelt knew a thing or two about courage. He was a paraplegic who might have wanted to hide away from society, but instead he led America through a world war and a great Depression.

THE MOUSE FEAR

'Fear of fear' – how does that work? Well, say you are afraid of mice. Quite apart from the fact that a mouse cannot harm you, there is something inherently strange about a phobia in that it recurs long after the original stimulus has gone. It goes on and on. It feeds on itself. Many musophobics cannot remember the first time they experienced the 'mouse fear'. It may have been a chance encounter with the little creature when they did not know what it was, or may have been an exposure to somebody *else*'s mouse fear – e.g. that of a parent. But having once felt it, they start to think about how frightened they were, and then to think of *ways to avoid that fear in future*. They begin to be afraid of the *idea* of mice and anything to do with mice – their tails, their shapes, their speed, their scurrying. Anything vaguely mouse-like now preys on their minds until the actual sight of the animal becomes a thing of pure terror. The original scare has grown out of all proportion until it invades consciousness itself. The whole experience of *mouse* becomes perilous, mind-threatening, overwhelming.

Yet the mouse has stayed the same. It is the fear that has grown.

How can this be? Let us revisit the poor musophobic long before he (or more probably she) began to jump on chairs at the first sight of a tiny tail. When the child first encounters the mouse, she may feel a small surge of apprehension at something unusual or not understood. If she has been told by somebody else that mice are frightening, the experience is all the more likely to trigger thoughts of a mouse 'threat'. Now, the child has two choices.

1   If she *goes towards* the mouse and examines it, and is not harmed, her level of fear goes down. Initial apprehension may be replaced by curiosity, by fascination or even compassion, so that she wishes to see *other* mice and find out all about them.

2   But if she *runs away*, her initial apprehension will not have reduced at all. She will not have learned anything about the mouse. It will be unknown, mysterious, potentially harmful. She will have had a wholly negative, scary experience. Running away causes a feedback loop: 'I must run faster, I am in danger, I may be chased.' The heart beats louder, the pulse quickens, the thoughts race: 'The peril is gaining on me, it is coming after me. I am really

frightened.' The fear itself is extremely unpleasant, and grows more unpleasant the more it is experienced. The child wishes to avoid such fear in the future. And so the mouse threat grows. And with every avoidance, it grows worse and more terrifying.

DESENSITISATION

What exactly *is* desensitisation? It means progressive exposure to the thing that frightens you, and to the *fear* you experience, in order to master it. Members of the armed forces are trained by progressive exposure so that they become 'seasoned' or hardened. An agoraphobic, on the other hand, has trained himself to avoid exposure altogether, until he is afraid to venture outside the front door. Unlike the hardened soldier, the agoraphobic has used avoidance of fear as a life tactic. Normal tasks and challenges causing a little apprehension, instead of being accepted, are avoided because of the fear involved. But then that fear, because it has been avoided, becomes an unknown quantity. Its quantity might be very great. It might unhinge the mind or prove fatal – the agoraphobic simply doesn't know. Apprehension therefore builds up about this fear, and the ability to cope with it. It attaches to all contact with the world that caused the original fear, and then to all actions leading up to that contact, and then to everything else, until finally the sufferer realises that he or she is completely disabled and asks for help.

One form of cognitive behavioural therapy that has been found effective in treating agoraphobics *is* desensitisation. Patients are asked by the therapist to grade their fear on a scale of one to ten as they try to perform certain tasks: going towards the door, grasping the door-handle, opening the door, and so on. They are asked to talk through their level of fear and observe it going up or down. Gradually they learn that they can cope with quite high levels and still go ahead with the task. And as they face and conquer these feelings, their levels of arousal go down. The patient becomes inured, or desensitised. He or she can then walk out of the front door like everybody else.

Fear as a source of terror

There are many examples of fears that induce fear. Take, for example, the man who is afraid of dental treatment. He has to have a tooth extracted, and the dentist tells him, 'I can either give you a local anaesthetic to numb the area, or I can give you a general anaesthetic. The latter carries risks, and one of these unfortunately is death.' The frightened patient thinks about his options, and then says: 'Knock me out.' Why? Because he is more afraid of his dental fear than he is of the risk of death under a general anaesthetic. Some dental practices now carry a sign warning of the risks of GA in dentistry and offer counselling to overcome dental chair terror. But some patients have extracted their own teeth rather than face their dentophobia.

GOING TOWARDS FEAR

All phobias gain their power from *being escaped from*. The more you run away, the less you wish to fight them another day. So if you want to reduce their power you must go towards, not run. *Going towards* triggers a *positive* feedback loop: 'I may be nervous, but I am also courageous. I am curious. Let's see what happens if I do this.' Fear is replaced by a rush of adrenalin, by excitement and exhilaration because you have dared, and this means you are not a 'coward in corners', but a brave person. You are living in the moment, instead of fearing the past and the future.

Consider trying fear in safety

Horror movies are designed to offer you fear in safety. If you have never watched one, try it. Ask for advice from experienced horror-watchers and start with a fairly 'tame' one. Then if you enjoy it you can 'build up'. Wes Craven, the director of Nightmare on Elm Street, put it like this: 'People come out like just chattering and laughing and slapping each other on the back ... enjoying themselves in some strange, wonderful, giddy way.'

PINNING DOWN YOUR FEARS

Even though you take challenges, you may still be afraid. But the more you go towards, the more that fear will reduce. You are turning and facing the mythical monster, and progressively robbing it of its power to frighten you. You may object that some phobias do not involve harmless stimuli like mice. Some concern stimuli with genuine danger attached. Yet even these fears, once examined, are often inaccurate or inappropriate. 'Fear of heights' is *really* fear of falling from heights. You can be high up and never fall. 'Fear of school' is *really* fear of repeating bad experiences that a child has had at school. 'Fear of flying' is *really* fear of crashing. You may fly hundreds of times and never crash, and so on. So it pays to examine exactly what you fear, and think of ways to reduce that fear rather than augment it.

TROUNCING FEAR: THE NATURE OF THE NINTH CHALLENGE

Your ninth challenge is therefore to confront something you yourself are afraid of. *Choose the fear you will trounce.* You are not *necessarily* going to hang-glide or free-fall out of a plane, but I have interviewed people who get enormous pleasure from these activities who were previously terrified of heights – one being former world hang-gliding and paragliding champion Judy Leden. Children instinctively plump for physical 'dares' because they provide such life-affirming buzzes. And West Lothian great grandmother Gean Hodsdon from Linlithgow finds extreme sports absolutely 'her scene'. Gean celebrated her 90th birthday in March 2010 by going white-water rafting down the River Tay. Asked what she thought of it afterwards, she said it was OK but that 'there were a lot of flat bits'.

You will appreciate the value of stepping outside your comfort zone by exploring the websites of the outdoor adventure organisations listed below.

Outdoor and adventure challenges
If you choose an outdoor or adventure challenge, here are some organisations that can help you. Go to their websites and feel the thrill:

The Institute for Outdoor Learning

Tel: 01228 564580; e-mail: institute@outdoor-learning.org

Based in Carlisle, Cumbria, the Institute gives access to properly accredited and experienced training providers and professional development schemes.

The Outward Bound Trust

Tel: 020 7610 4218; website at: outwardboundtrust.org.uk

Since 1941 over a million young people have taken part in one of their outdoor activity schemes. They provide adventure holidays and personal development programmes to excite and motivate 11- to 24-year-olds as well as adult corporate programmes.

The Duke of Edinburgh's Award

Tel: 01753 727400; e-mail: info@DofE.org for regional offices

The youth charity has adventure and development programmes for young people between the ages of 14 and 24 who receive awards for completing four or five challenge sections.

PSYCHOLOGICAL DARES

Your own chosen 'fear to trounce' may not be of any physical experience at all. It may be purely psychological. You may be petrified of speaking to your boss. You may be mortified and have to visit the toilet repeatedly at the thought of going to the dentist, or speaking in public, or going on a blind date. It is up to you to choose a fear that you wish to confront. But first, let's understand properly what we are trying to achieve by looking at *other people's* phobias.

Phobia List Exercise

Look through the list of phobias at the start of the chapter and devise a challenge for every phobia on the list. In each case:

- *Explain how to confront that particular fear.*

- *Decide whether to set a gradual or sudden challenge.*

- *What is to be thought through before the event?*

- *What is the real level of danger?*

- *How would you help the phobic to distinguish between the real danger and the threat perceived?*

- *What would you tell the phobic to encourage (to give courage to) him or her?*

Now choose your own fear and set out your own programme of progress towards fearlessness. Good luck, but do you know what? You won't need it.

KEEP A RECORD OF YOUR CHALLENGE HERE

Fear challenged:

Date:

Time:

Preparation:

How I felt prior:

How I felt after:

What I learned about the nature of fear:

WHAT PANEL MEMBERS THOUGHT

Katey

'My problem is I can't afford to go on any adventure activities, but I did a scary dare. I went to a little zoo where they let you go in and handle the reptiles. I touched a chameleon which was quite rough and spiky, but the main, amazing thing was that I had a bloody great snake draped round my shoulders. It was amazingly heavy, but not slimy at all – which was the thing that horrified me before I actually did it. It kept looking at me and I suddenly thought: "You're just an animal. You're really beautiful." Afterwards you feel quite calm about everything and what a wuss you've been for years and maybe you should try more things.'

Vaz

'You finally threw me a curve this time. I couldn't get out of this one as I'm quite capable of doing sports and outdoor things. I've just been a bit down and a bit lazy. Cut a very long story short, we went up to Derbyshire in my mate's four-by-four with his two bikes on the back. We cycled round the area and we got round to going up the bottoms of a few slopes. He's like a goat but I had to do it very gingerly. It was *great. Absolutely.* I know I can be a prick sometimes – it's just a cover. If I'm honest, I want to do something better than I've been doing, going out and getting smashed with stupid superficial traders and falling flat on my face. I want to do something more valuable. I think now I will. You find out stuff by doing this stuff.'

Charlotte

'I don't like anybody seeing me even semi-dressed, but I've always wanted to go swimming as I used to when I was a kid and I loved the sea. So I thought: what can I do that's halfway like the thing I really want to do? With swimming there's nothing really. You either do it or don't. So I bought this *very* nice costume, and even trying that on in the fitting room I was petrified in case anybody came in. I haven't worn it yet. But now I've got it, it will play on my mind. Does that count? If it makes you excited it must do.'

Barbara

'I had my teeth done! Since I was married I let my teeth go because I kept putting it at the bottom of the list like you do. Then when I did make an appointment I would cancel it. I took a friend with me this time and read the magazines and wouldn't speak to her, but I thought: "If I walk out of here now I'm never going to do it." I hated the needle but it lasted a couple of seconds and then you don't feel a thing. We came out of there and I felt as if I'd fought my fear and won. Anyone else would probably think: how boring is that!'

Terry

'I tried a couple of little challenges I won't bore you with as they weren't particularly scary – bad horror flicks, having a tattoo and such. People will probably think I'm a prat as I can't afford it, but I've really always wanted to go up in a hot air balloon. I've got the leaflet. It's expensive, so my new girlfriend bought me one of these pig money boxes as she says I could save on other things – by which no doubt she means my fag and drink money. She says if it takes me a month, or a couple of months, so what? And she's got a point. Life is ******* short and you're only here once. Why not go for it? So far I'm a third of the way up there.'

George

'I went on the Institute for Outdoor Learning website and got in touch with them and there are several things I want to do. I did a bit of sailing when I was a lad and it appeals to me. I wouldn't have considered any of this if I hadn't done the other challenges first. You couldn't really just jump into it. It's a big learning curve for me but I reckon if you're depressed, this is the way forward. It's no good sitting in a heap any more.'

Ten: the life challenge

If you have worked your way through the other nine challenges, you will now be ready to tackle the ultimate challenge: that of fulfilling a long-cherished ambition. Once you have found the courage to face the monster, to think hard about dumping drugs and dependencies and to rejoice in your own singularity, *most things do become possible*. I speak from experience: given the right psychological skills and the opportunity to practise them, even the most timid, self-constrained and despairing person can see through the glass ceiling and aim for the stars.

Remember the first challenge, when I asked you to think of things you've always wanted to do that you felt you ought to be *able* to do? Remember how I asked you to brainstorm possible methods of achieving them? Go back and look at the list now. You might choose one of those. Or you might select something more fundamental, or more ambitious.

First, let's find out about your dreamscape.

Dreamscape postcard exercise

Take a blank postcard (or any piece of card that is blank on both sides). The aim of this exercise is to design and write a holiday postcard, with a scene on the front bearing the message, 'Wish you were here.' It is addressed to somebody you haven't seen for a while.

When you've drawn your dreamscape (a simple cartoon style will do) on the back you write to your friend. But the card is not just wishful thinking. It has to explain HOW YOU GOT THERE.

THE SLOW SEDATION OF WANTS

What generally stops people from getting to their goals? The deadness. The numbing of desire. The gradual erosion of their dreams from constant rejection and disappointment, until all they can say is 'Oh, it doesn't matter.' It *does* matter. Your dreams *do* matter, and this book was written to help you achieve them. But you need to realise that most people don't reach their dreams because they don't *want* them enough. In many ways, despair is the culmination of this slow sedation of wants and wishes.

Consider the opposite case – that of a ghetto kid who desperately wants to be a boxing champion. Every morning when his brown eyes flick open, the first thing he sees in his mind is himself in the ring, glistening with sweat, getting away from his impoverished, slum-bum background and punching his way to glory. He wants it so much he can *taste* it. This is what's known in the fight game as 'hunger'. Without it, nobody succeeds. With it, anyone can overcome apparently insurmountable odds. Now, aside from the fact that you may be appalled that this child wants to devote his life to violence, what's the difference between him and you?

The ghetto kid

- *has no choice because he can't afford to fail*

- *is desperate to succeed so he is focused*

- *doesn't have the luxury of saying I'll do it tomorrow*

- *is therefore under time pressure*

- *is therefore uninhibited*

- *is willing to risk making a fool of himself*

- *has nothing to lose.*

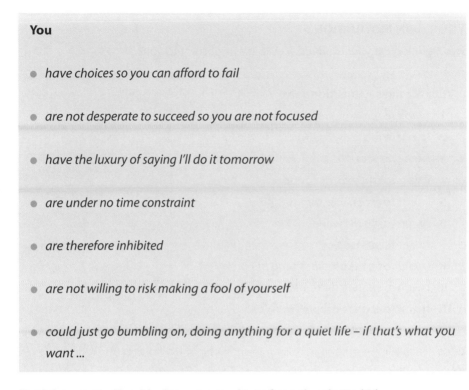

You

- *have choices so you can afford to fail*

- *are not desperate to succeed so you are not focused*

- *have the luxury of saying I'll do it tomorrow*

- *are under no time constraint*

- *are therefore inhibited*

- *are not willing to risk making a fool of yourself*

- *could just go bumbling on, doing anything for a quiet life – if that's what you want ...*

Don't be snooty. Consider how you can learn from the ghetto kid.

YOUR OWN MOTIVATION

Now let's look at *your* motivation. What's important to you?

Your Motives – Questionnaire

  1   *I want to make money.*

  2   *I want to make my mark.*

  3   *I want respect.*

  4   *I want to stay exactly as I am.*

  5   *I want to experience things.*

  6   *I want to see the world.*

  7   *I want to be loved.*

  8   *I want to be the best that I can be.*

  9   *I want to change the world.*

10   *I want to change people's minds.*

11   *I want to succeed for my family.*

When you have decided on your answers, consider this: **only 5 and 8 do not depend on other people**. They can hurt you. So if you didn't choose 5 or 8 be prepared for rejection and disappointment and don't be put off when you get them. If we go for our goals, we generally get hurt. Be ready for that. *It is still worth it.*

One of the most important exercises I did with my classes was to put a plastic chair out in front with a sign on the seat. It was a big sign. It said three words:

WHAT I WANT

I would stand talking about motivation to my trainees, sometimes deliberately positioning myself in front of the sign so they couldn't see it. Life is like that. People stand in front of your dreams and obscure them from view. I told my trainees to keep focusing on the sign, and eventually they would be able to see it again. Then I would ask them, one by one, to leave the room (we found this was symbolically important), knock on the door to gain admittance, say their name, even though we knew who they were, walk over to the WHAT I WANT chair, and sit in it. Then they had to tell us what they actually wanted to do, what their real ambitions were, how they had tried and failed and so on. If they seemed hesitant the class would fire questions at them. If they bullshitted us by saying things like 'I want to go home' or 'I want to go to the pub' we would shuck that aside and carry on questioning. Using this simple, stark technique we would usually get to the bottom of what they really wanted fairly quickly. Most people know in their hearts what they want. They just get scared of saying it out loud, and then they get scared of thinking it.

What do you want? Say it out loud. Think it. *Keep* thinking it. Now you're on the right track.

DREAMS AND GOALS

What's the difference between a dream and a goal? The answer is this.

A dream is a pie in the sky.
A goal is a plan on the planet.

On the following page you will find a chart. I've printed it very large as it is very important. I want you to fill it out as carefully and as honestly as you can. In the top *left*-hand corner you list your **dreams**, in order of preference. In the top *right*-hand corner I want you to list your **goals**. You know the difference? Goals are dreams with some muscle behind them. Goals are more realistic than dreams because you take action to make them happen. In fact, that's the main difference. In fact that's the *only* difference!

Which things on your list are you prepared to work towards? What are the steps you are going to take to help you achieve these objectives? If you think hard enough and clearly enough, you may be able to transfer things from your left column to your right column. List your affirmative actions underneath.

DREAM LIST (*hopes with no backup*)	**GOAL LIST** (*hopes with backup*)
1st	1st
2nd	2nd
3rd	3rd
4th	4th
5th	5th
6th	6th
Actions to help Dreams	**Actions to support Goals**

Now take the final challenge. Choose the very top goal on your list, the one that is most important to you. *Go for your goal.* The sooner you start, and the more you work at it, the sooner you will succeed.

TAKING THE PLEDGE

I hope you've enjoyed this book. I believe the challenges will change you. They will make you stronger, both mentally and physically, and they will vanquish your despair. So long as you take action to help yourself, despair cannot disable you. So long as you make plans on the planet and work towards them, despair cannot numb your motivation. Know what you want, face the monster, be courageous. Never turn away and just look for the quiet life. You've tried that and you didn't like it. Keep daring, keep trying until you succeed. Make your world a real world instead of a psychological prison.

Before I leave, I'm going to ask you to do what I asked all my candidates to do on our Restart courses, and that is to *take the pledge* on the next page. If you take it, I'll know you're serious about turning your life around and challenging despair. I'll know that you're not prepared to suffer it or put up with it any more.

Much more important, *you* will know.

The pledge is not a document that you will need to show to anybody else. It's strictly private, between you and your brain. Do take it. Do mean it.
Good luck – but you know what? That's exactly right. You won't need it!

Angela Patmore

SOLEMN UNDERTAKING BETWEEN MYSELF AND MY BRAIN

LIFE GOAL

....

SPECIAL OBJECTIVES

....
....
....

ACTIONS TO SUPPORT

....
....
....
....

IDEAS TO SUPPORT

....
....
....
....

I swear by things I hold dear that I will now use my brain to fulfil my potential. I swear that I will not waste my life or my talent and that from now on I will do my best to honour my ambitions and myself.

Signed ....

Dated ....

Index